Sointula

Sointula

ISLAND UTOPIA

PAULA WILD

HARBOUR

Harbour Publishing
Box 219
Madeira Park, BC
Canada VON 2HO
www.harbourpublishing.com

Page design by Lionel Trudel, Aspect Design.
Cover & author photos by Rick James.
Map on page 8 by Lionel Trudel, Aspect Design
Photo credit abbreviations: SM—Sointula Museum, BCARS—Brit-
ish Columbia Archives and Records Service, SC—Sointula Co-op,
NM—Nanaimo District Museum
Printed and bound in Canada.

Published with the assistance of the Canada Council and the Province of British Columbia through the British Columbia Arts Council.

THE CANADA COUNCIL | LE CONSEIL DES ARTS
FOR THE ARTS | DU CANADA
SINCE 1957 | DEPUIS 1957

BRITISH
COLUMBIA
ARTS COUNCIL
Supported by the Province of British Columbia

Canadian Cataloguing in Publication Data

Wild, Paula
  Sointula

  Includes bibliographical references and index.
  ISBN 1-55017-128-3 (bound).—ISBN 978-1-55017-456-4 (pbk.)
  1. Sointula (B.C.)—History. I. Title.
FC3849.S64W54 1995   971.1'2   95-910417-8   FI089.5.S64W54 1995

This book is dedicated to the memory of Tauno Salo, a man of *sisu*,

and

to Rick James for his assistance with research, photography, and editing, for reading innumerable drafts, and for more or less putting up with the piles of paper that accumulated throughout the past six years.

I would like to thank all the people who generously shared their time, personal histories and family albums with me while I was researching *Sointula: Island Utopia*.

Their help was invaluable; without their words this book would not exist. I am especially indebted to Matti Linnoila for his assistance with photographs and information about his great grandfather, Matti Kurikka.

The language barrier was a difficult one to surmount. The Finns who settled Malcolm Island left many written records, but Finnish is not an easy language to read. Using a Finnish-English dictionary was cumbersome; hiring a professional translator was expensive. So I asked people to translate for me, passing out pages of documents and letters, often not having the faintest idea what they were about.

It wasn't easy to find people who not only were interested in the project and had the time to devote to it, but who were also capable of reading Finnish and writing English. As one of my translators, Anja Auer pointed out, "Finnish is a very curly language-it is hard to find words in English that express the same feeling." Anja and my other translators frequently commented on the Finnish settlers' beautiful handwriting, the sentence structure that indicated an advanced education, and above all, the Finns' love of Sointula. Tauno Salo and Ted and Janet Tanner often added their personal memories to the translations, allowing a detailed story to spring from an old piece of paper.

Thank you Anja Auer, Violet Bokstrom, Tuula Lewis, Loretta Rihtamo, Tauno and Ruth Salo, and especially Janet and Ted Tanner, who not only translated but also acted as an "information bureau" for my countless questions.

Sointula

ISLAND UTOPIA

TABLE OF CONTENTS

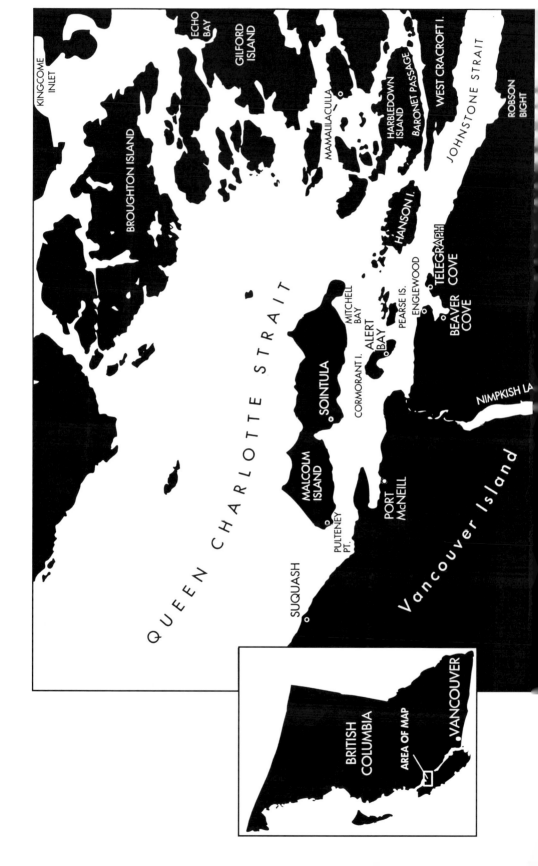

"It was the centre of the world
for me and the world was
revolving around it."

Aino Ahola

Looking For a Better Life

THROUGHOUT THE AGES, A DESIRE FOR A SENSE of self and a sense of place has motivated the human race to search for a better life. The sixteenth century writer and philosopher, Sir Thomas More, defined this yearning in his book *Utopia*. More chose the word "utopia" to signify a point midway between *outopia* (no place) and *eutopia* (the good place). Thus the word utopia refers not to a specific location, but to an ideal state where harmony exists between individuals as well as between society and nature.

More's concept of utopia was based on the belief that people were capable of creating their own destinies. He placed his utopia on an island shaped like a crescent moon.

Public lectures were held daily and intellectual pursuits, music and conversation were highly regarded. Fundamental principles included communal property, labour and dining. More believed that "Each meal taken together stands for the triumph of justice and represents the equality and communion of all citizens." Later utopian concepts often included celibacy or free love, and placed an emphasis on physical labour and exercise.

Utopias require physical and social boundaries. A conscious effort is made to separate from mainstream society and to establish a private place removed from outside influences. Utopians value their coherence as a group, and what takes place within the community is sharply differentiated from what happens outside of it. Utopia provides an escape from the past, and the promise of a future where meaningful lives are more important than material wealth.

Since More's time, utopias have appeared on a regular basis. They were particularly popular around the turn of the nineteenth century, when they were seen as a practical and adventuresome alternative to the upheaval caused by the industrial and urban revolutions in Europe. North America, with its vast lands and flexible social structures, seemed to present unlimited possibilities. As the most western province of Canada, British Columbia was a magnet for a variety of dreamers, idealists and utopians. Religious sects such as the Doukhobors and Mennonites settled in isolated pockets on the mainland, while small groups of Norwegians and Danes attempted to establish communities in the Bella Coola Valley and Cape Scott on north Vancouver Island.

Islands, with natural boundaries that favour refuge and retreat, have been favourite locations for utopian communities. Nestled between the mainland and the northern end of Vancouver Island, Malcolm Island has been the site of several utopian ventures. Since the late 1800s people of all ages, nationalities and occupations have moved to the island in search of a better life. An English religious group, socialist Finns, and disillusioned North Americans form the backbone of Malcolm Island's utopian heritage, but it is the Finns who have most clearly impressed their character on the island. Like many experimental communities, the Finns' official utopia failed. For most idealistic colonies, the end of the communal effort was the end of the dream. But the Finns were more persistent. A group of them remained on Malcolm Island to forge a viable community that still thrives today.

Unlike traditional west coast settlements, the people came to Malcolm Island first, before the industry. Arvo Tynjala, an early member of the Finnish utopian commune on the island, summed it up: "Most communities, whatever they are—

little towns or villages—they're usually formed around some kind of industrial development, either a logging camp, a pulp-mill, or a sawmill. But in Sointula it was different. The people went there on their own and then started to build the community. It took some courage you know, to go into the wilderness and build a community without any help."

Mink Builds a Mountain

MOST PEOPLE COME TO MALCOLM ISLAND BY choice rather than chance. Approximately 24 kilometres (15 miles) long and three kilometres (two miles) wide at its deepest point, the island lies between Broughton Strait and the southern end of Queen Charlotte Strait. Today, travel by vehicle from Vancouver requires two ferry rides and a four- to five-hour drive up the east coast of Vancouver Island. At Campbell River, the highway leaves the sea and winds through a largely unpopulated patchwork of second growth forest and vast logged areas. From the logging town of Port McNeill, a small ferry makes a triangular run to Malcolm and Cormorant islands. For those with less time and more money, the island is also accessible by float plane or helicopter.

In the nineteenth century, access to Malcolm Island was limited to travel by water. The island received its name in 1846 when the sidewheel steamer HMS *Cormorant* was investigating reports of large coal deposits on northern Vancouver Island. Commander George T. Gordon called the island Malcolm in honour of Admiral Sir Pulteney Malcolm of the Royal Navy, who was well known and liked, both for his pleasant manner and his spirit and skill in battle. A nearby island, on which the community of Alert Bay is now located, was named *Cormorant* after the vessel itself.

Long before the *Cormorant* passed Malcolm Island however, others were familiar with its shores. Malcolm Island is located in the midst of Kwakwaka'wakw territory. Kwakwaka'wakw culture did not originally include land as private property. Instead, each band owned the rights to various fishing and berry-picking grounds and migrated between them as the seasons changed. Ethnologist Franz Boas visited this area many times between 1886 and 1931. He identified a dozen Kwakwaka'wakw place names on Malcolm Island and documented that several family groups owned over twenty halibut fishing locations near the east side of the island. The presence of stone tools, shell middens and petroglyphs indicate that Malcolm Island was a regular seasonal home of the Kwakwaka'wakw.

Lacking a written language, the Kwakwaka'wakw used rock carvings to recognize important people, places or events, and to record fishing locations, property rights, freshwater springs, myths and shaman sites. Normally these carvings were located near a village, the mouth of a stream, or in an isolated place where secret ceremonies took place. Fort Rupert natives told Boas that the first petroglyphs were created "before animals turned into men."

Malcolm Island's largest petroglyph is located on a north shore beach near Lizard Point. Approximately one-and-a-half metres (five feet) wide and three metres (10 feet) long, the granite boulder is partially buried in gravel and features a circle face with prominent eyes and thick eyebrows that appear to meet over the nose. The rock slopes towards the sea and the lower mouth section has been noticeably eroded by waves over time. Ray and Beth Hill, authors of *Indian Petroglyphs of the Pacific Northwest*, discovered a freshwater spring under the stone. In Kwakwaka'wakw legend springs were often used by shamans to access the power or sexual energy of nature. Behind the petroglyph, above the beach is a small stand of gnarled crab apple trees and a midden containing clam shells and barnacles. This site was known to natives on Village Island, who claimed that it was once a good clamming area and for this reason it may have been the site of an old village.

Additional petroglyphs are located in the intertidal zone in front of the cliffs that form Donegal Head on the eastern tip of the island. These drawings, consisting of circle faces and a series of eyes, are among the most common found on the coast. Circle faces are thought to represent the shaman involved in a salmon ceremony, while eyes are believed to portray spirits.

While non-native local legend says that natives do not live on Malcolm Island because the island is going to sink, the Kwakwaka'wakw told Boas a different story. G·ē´xk·în of Nimpkish River said that long ago Mink, an important character in Kwakwaka'wakw mythology, paddled to Malcolm Island in his canoe. After exploring the island, Mink decided to make it his home, but was disappointed because there were

no mountains. Determined to create his own mountain, Mink dug up spruce roots and split them to make a basket, which he filled with gravel from the beach. Day after day Mink carried loads of gravel to the center of the is-

A rubbing of the petroglyph at Lizard Point taken by Alfred Williams, late 1970s. (Rick James; SM)

land, where he dumped them in a big pile. When the mountain nearly reached the clouds, he took four days off to collect salmonberry, huckleberry, and elderberry bushes. Mink planted these bushes on the mountain and began to haul more gravel. But now, every time he emptied his basket the stones ran down the side of the mountain. Mink got very angry and kicked the rocks apart until all that remained of his mountain was a hill. After a while Mink calmed down and decided to stay on the island after all. That, the Kwakwaka'wakw say, is why Malcolm Island has lots of mink and no mountains.

After European contact introduced the concept of private property, twenty-one young men from the Kwakulth Band at Fort Rupert on Vancouver Island requested that Indian Reserve Commissioner, A. W. Vowell, grant them 320 acres on the east side of Malcolm Island's Rough Bay. Their letter, dated March 1890, stated that land at Fort Rupert was limited and that many of them were forced to rent property from the Hunt family. (When the Hudson's Bay Company left Fort Rupert in 1873, resident agent Robert Hunt bought the property. He, and later his descendants, rented out portions of the land.) In their letter the Kwakulth also complained that canoe access to Fort Rupert was difficult except at extreme high tide, and impossible during a southeasterly wind, which blew for nine months of the year. On Malcolm Island they hoped to begin a new life farming and raising cattle. Although Indian Agent Reginald Pidcock forwarded the letter to Vowell with his full endorsement, the Kwakulths' request was denied. Twenty-six years later the Royal Commission on Indian Affairs, commonly known as the McKenna-McBride Commission, granted the Kwakwaka'wakw a 480-acre land-locked parcel near Pulteney Point for farming and general purposes.

European settlement of Malcolm Island began in 1883 with the pre-emption of over 500 acres near Mitchell Bay by William Clarke and Charles McHardy. An October 1890 diary entry by Rev. A. W. Corker, a Protestant minister of the

Church Missionary Society stationed at Fort Rupert, mentions attending a lecture at Malcolm Island with "35 white people present." A rancher named Circero Charles Williams obtained one hundred acres in Rough Bay in 1893. He was joined two years later by the Christian Temperance Commonwealth Society, an English religious sect led by penitential clergyman Joseph Spencer, a visionary who dreamed of creating a utopian Christian commune. Spencer had gathered a small following and purchased a sawmill, steam plant and engine from Vancouver Island coal baron James Dunsmuir. The group travelled to Malcolm Island by steamship, towing their possessions behind on a flatbed barge. Their first night on the island was a miserable one. Adam Mathers, who later moved to the mouth of the Nimpkish River, recalled: "All our food, clothing, and household goods were on the barge and completely soaked by waves. There was no shelter so my wife and I slept under a tree holding our youngest children against our bare breasts to keep them warm." The next day the settlers dried their belongings and began to build a board cabin, and clear fields by hand. After only a few months of this back-breaking work the society dissolved.

At the same time that Spencer's group was struggling to establish its commune, E. Elliman, an immigrant from Denmark, quit his job as foreman at a wood-processing plant in San Francisco. An educated man who frequently travelled abroad, Elliman was disillusioned with the false values of civilization and longed for a simple life. He found what he was looking for on the south side of Malcolm Island, where he built a cabin beside a small creek, grew vegetables and raised chickens. In the summer of 1901 a native from nearby Cormorant Island found him dead on the beach. Elliman had been the last of the settlers; Spencer's group, Williams, Clarke and McHardy had all abandoned their homesteads some time ago.

CHAPTER TWO

The Kalevala

T WELFTH-CENTURY FINLAND WAS A COUNTRY of many tribes, loosely connected by their unique language and a complex mythology, emphasizing harmony with nature, that was communicated by song. In the mid 1500s, Finland became a pawn in the political and territorial struggles between Sweden and Russia. For the next three hundred years, the two countries battled on Finnish soil, until finally in 1809 the country was ceded to Russia. At first, life under Russian rule was good. Finns were granted self-government, their own army, and freedom of language. As they gained a sense of national pride and identity, folk songs and legends became a popular way to express their patriotism.

Elias Lönnrot, a small-town physician and classical scholar, was captivated by the folk song-poems called runes. He began collecting and combining them in a manner similar to Homer's *Iliad*. When he finished, Lönnrot had created a rune 12,000 lines long which he called the *Kalevala*.

Kalevala, the land of heroes, is the name of a mythical part of Finland which is engaged in a continuous struggle with Pohjola, the evil land of the north. Published in 1835, the *Kalevala* soon became a national folk epic. Though unpolitical in content, it became highly political in influence, stimulating Finnish nationalism and reinforcing the uniqueness of the

Finnish language.

When Finland industrialized in the 1860s, rural residents flooded the labour market, creating a new social class—the migrant worker—that was especially vulnerable to economic depression and famine. Trade unions began to appear, and in 1895 the daily newspaper Tyomies (Worker) was established. Then Nicholas II became Czar of Russia, and life in Finland changed radically. Russian was declared the official language, and Finnish legislation and the post office were placed under Russian rule. The Czar's February 1899 manifesto increased censorship of the press and introduced a new conscription law, making it mandatory for Finns to serve a five-year term in the Russian army. Failure to abide by the Bobrikov Examinations, as the rules of censorship were called, resulted in jailor exile to Siberia.

Organized Finn workers founded a separate political party which advocated the right to vote, an eight-hour work day and education for the masses. The party was in sharp conflict with the Lutheran Church, which at that time opposed universal education, land tenure reform and trade unions. Leaders of the socialist movement became political exiles, and many Finns carried their passports in their pockets, ready to flee at a moment's notice. Having experienced the exhilaration of cultural growth and nationalism, they were determined to have a nation of their own, even if they had to travel outside the boundaries of their homeland to find it.

The exodus from Finland took workers to Sweden, Australia and North America. Finns began emigrating to Canada in 1882 to work on the transcontinental Canadian Pacific Railway. Jobs were plentiful, and the new immigrants wrote to friends and family encouraging them to emigrate also. When railway construction was finished in eastern Canada, most of the Finns found other jobs in Ontario, the United States and British Columbia. In British Columbia they split into two groups, one going to the interior to farm and work on railway construction, the other moving to Vancouver Island to work in the coal mines near Nanaimo.

While the mines provided steady employment, conditions were grim. Many of the Finns were hired to push tram cars loaded with ore for $3.00 a day. During their ten- to twelve-hour shift they worked underground in perpetual darkness, with the constant threat of fire, cave-ins and death from afterdamp, the lethal gas created when coal dust explodes. Between 1899 and 1908, twenty-three men died for every million tons of coal produced in British Columbia. "To know the toil and burdensomeness of descending into the bottomless jaws, never knowing whether one will surface alive, dead, or badly injured to live the rest of one's life a cripple at the mercy of

James Dunsmuir was known to Vancouver Island coal miners as the "millionaire and skinner of men." (BCARS 78887)

others," was Finnish miner Matti Halminen's description of working in the mines.

Above ground, life wasn't much better. Rough wooden shacks were called home, few women were present and little existed in the way of social activities. A popular source of solace was the tavern located near each mining settlement. Mine owner, and premier of British Columbia from June 1900 to November 1902, James Dunsmuir encouraged drinking by allowing two breweries to make wagon deliveries to the camp each day and letting the miners charge their purchases against their monthly pay cheque. Drinking and fighting were often the only entertainment, and any attempts by the miners to improve living or working conditions were immediately thwarted by Dunsmuir. To compound their problems, even though many of the Finns were well educated, they experienced great difficulty with the English language. Linguistically Finnish differs from all European languages except Estonian and early Magyar. Finnish has no articles, prepositions or gender, and the letters b, c, f, q and w do not exist. Word endings may change to signify singular or plural, positive or negative, and formal or familiar. Finnish also possesses a large number of words to describe similar but different meanings. The sound of the wind in pine trees is *humista* while the same sound heard in birch trees is *kohista*, and neither word is interchangeable. Culturally isolated and unable to communicate, the Finns were frequently called "stupid Russian foreigners," which inevitably led to more drinking and fighting.

Deeply disappointed in the new world and looking for ways to improve their life, a group of Finnish miners living near Nanaimo at Wellington formed the Lannen Rusko (Western Glow) on February 5, 1890. It was the first Finnish temperance society in Canada, and its goal was to unite Finns, provide insurance and aid for the sick and injured, and discourage the consumption of alcohol. An abandoned building in Wellington's Chinatown was repaired to use as a meeting place. "A modest hall," Halminen recalled, "but meetings so brotherly and engrossing that even after forty years they linger in memory."

On October 11, 1891, a group of Finns met at the home of Jaako Rajala and formed another temperance society called the *Aallotar* (Water Nymph). The most progressive temperance society of its time, the *Aallotar* soon had a meeting hall and reading room, and with the assistance of the *Lännen Rusko*, began a Finnish language library and a brass hand. This was the beginning of spiritual awakening for the Finns in North America. They built comfortable homes, discussed living and working conditions and began to gain the respect of the English-speaking population.

Then Dunsmuir began mining coal nineteen kilometres (twelve miles) away at Extension. To keep their jobs, the miners were forced to dismantle their shacks and move them to the new location. Not long afterwards Dunsmuir formed the town of Ladysmith on Oyster Harbour, where coal from Extension was loaded onto the ships. Once again workers were expected to move at their own expense, and this time to purchase building lots from Dunsmuir. Tired of Dunsmuir's callousness and abuse, Halminen and many of the other Finns longed to quit the mines. But jobs were scarce and no one had much in the way of money. A group of twenty Finns were involved in socialism, and during a discussion on ways to improve living and working conditions they suggested forming a utopian, socialist community.

It was early 1900 when Aatami Korhonen, Viljo Jokinen, and Heikki Kilpeläinen arrived in Wellington from Queensland, Australia. With them they brought pamphlets written by Finnish expatriate and utopian idealist Matti Kurikka. Excited about what they read, the Finns asked Halminen, a hard-working, serious man, to write to Kurikka. On April 8, Halminen sent a letter to Australia asking Kurikka to come to Canada and lead them to a new life.

CHAPTER THREE

An Impractical Faddist

MATTI KURIKKA WAS BORN IN 1863 AND RAISED near St. Petersburg, a part of Finland that was alternately dominated by Sweden and Russia. His parents, deeply religious and originally wealthy land owners, were forced to become peasants and considered themselves lucky not to be conscripted into the Russian army or put into jail. While attending the University of Helsinki, Kurikka became involved with Minna Canth, a novelist and suffragette, who was a leader in the revival of the Finnish language. Canth's strong personality had a powerful impact on Kurikka. Nearly twenty years his senior, she introduced him to the works of Tolstoy, cultivated his interest in idealism and welcomed him as a member of her literary salon. From Canth, a widow with seven children, Kurikka absorbed a feminist philosophy on marriage, women's rights and the raising of children.

At the age of twenty-three Kurikka married Anna Palmqvist, the beautiful daughter of a wealthy Helsinki family. The newlyweds spent the next couple of years travelling in Europe with the Palmqvists, where for the first time Kurikka was directly exposed to socialism and the conditions of the working class. When he returned to Finland, Kurikka found a sounding board for his socialist beliefs as editor, shareholder and eventual owner of the popular Finnish newspaper the Viipurin *Sanomat* (Viipurin News). Pro-labour and anti-establishment, Kurikka focused his editorials on the status and education of women and the value and dignity of physical labour. Eventually he left the Sanomat to become editor of the working class newspaper, Tyomies. There he wrote articles on everything from Buddhism to industry, and renewed his ties with Austin Mäkelä, an old university friend and supporter of Minna Canth.

A recurring theme in Kurikka's writing was the distinction between true Christianity and the established church. Though he often condemned Christianity as a negative, "shalt not" religion, he was always careful to direct his barbs toward church officials rather than the concept of Christianity. True Christianity, he believed, was based on the teachings of Christ and should be the supreme guide in life. To Kurikka, Christ was positive and invigorating, the first and most enlightened socialist.

As well as a labour journalist, Kurikka was also well known

Matti Kurikka, Finnish socialist and visionary, in Finland, circa 1893. By the age of 30 Kurikka had established himself as a labour journalist and playwright. Many of his articles advocated women's rights; his plays often criticized the tyranny of the Lutheran Church. (Daniel Nyblin; Linnoila collection)

Matti Kurikka and his first wife Anna, circa 1886. Anna came from a wealthy Helsinki family. Kurikka was passionate, intelligent and charismatic, but in the end, too much of an impractical dreamer for the marriage to continue.
(Daniel Nyblin; Linnoila collection)

as a playwright. He was only twenty-one when his first play, *Viimeinen Ponnistus* (The Last Struggle), a drama highlighting the conflict between social classes, was produced to favourable reviews. Fifteen years later, in 1899, he presented his latest play to a friend who was also the manager of a large theatre in Helsingfors. *The Tower of Babel* harshly portrayed the decadence of religious and political hierarchies. "For too long the Priesthood has pandered to the lower instincts of man and prevented the liberty of thought," Kurikka wrote. "Their destruction is near. There they are now, like The Tower of Babel, falling into ruin in the midst of their iniquity." It took Kurikka several hours to convince his friend to put on the play. Opening night was a disaster, and *The Tower of Babel*'s first performance was also its last. The audience was outraged and Kurikka was deluged with criticism. Although he swore, "I would have written that play over again with my life's blood if I thought I could have improved

A political meeting in Viipurin, Finland, 1899. From left to right: K.K. Nord, Matti Kurikka, J.A. Lyly, E.J. Roini, Austin Mäkelä. Friends since university, Kurikka and Mäkelä worked together on several newspapers in Finland. Kurikka was a flamboyant personality always on centre stage; Mäkelä was a quiet, practical man content to remain in the background. (SM)

it," his career as a popular playwright was finished.

At this time Kurikka was experiencing personal problems as well as public humiliations. For years his brother-in-law had criticized his wild imagination and now even his wife was fed up with his dreamy and idealistic nature. The Kurikkas amicably divorced, Anna taking custody of their eleven-year-old daughter Aili. *The Tower of Babel*, the divorce, and Kurikka's growing involvement with theosophy, a religious philosophy that preached love, freedom and harmony with nature through mystical insight, completely severed his ties with upper-class Helsinki.

Devoting himself to socialism, Kurikka began a series of

articles on the topic. He became closely linked with the working-class movement, not as a Marxist but as an idealist who saw economics as merely a base for the cultural awakening necessary to free Finns from the yoke of Russia. To Kurikka, the Marxist theory that social structure should be controlled by the working class emphasized hate and bitterness. He referred to Marxists as "stomach socialists," saying, "People become socialist in two ways, through the head, or through the stomach." Effective reform, Kurikka believed, came from the heart, not from violent revolution. Advocating a society formed on the power of love, justice and humanity, he argued: "Love develops and creates, hate can only destroy."

By now a prominent figure in the socialist movement, Kurikka was recognized as a leader in the Finnish Socialist Federation. He fully expected to be elected as a director to the party at the electoral convention in 1899, but young radicals in the Marxist wing organized against him and he was ignored. Deeply disappointed and concerned by the acceleration of Russi-

Matti Kurikka with his seven-year-old daughter Alli in Finland, 1895. Even though the Kurikkas separated in 1899, Kurrika remained close to Alli and wrote to her frequently. (Daniel Nyblin; Linnoila collection)

fication, in particular the February manifesto of the Czar and the press censorship that went with it, Kurikka began campaigning for emigration. In one of his last articles as editor of the Tyomies, where his views on spiritualism and idealism were becoming unpopular with the paper's Marxist supporters, he proclaimed: "We shall discover the historical salvation of our people through emigration. In Finland the working class may eat only raw herring and drink skimmed milk . . . it is not worthwhile for working people to remain. I intend to move from the contamination and slander of Helsinki to a place where I may feel direct contact with nature."

At this time the Australian government was encouraging immigration from Finland and Scandinavia. This, plus the fact that the Australian government was pro-labour, convinced Kurikka to move there. In two public meetings that attracted over 800 people, he outlined a plan for a utopian society called the Kalevan Kansa (The People of Kaleva), where work, education and entertainment would be experienced communally. He said, "In this colony a high cultural life of freedom will be built away from priests, away from churches, and away from all the evils of the outside world."

A tall man with thick, black hair and blazing dark eyes, Kurikka knew how to capture the attention of his audience. He began speaking in a soft, slow voice, gradually becoming passionate and animated until he was striding about the stage and waving his arms dramatically. His enthusiasm was inspiring and contagious. Well aware of his personal magnetism and persuasive capabilities, Kurikka was not surprised when— immediately after the second meeting—the Kalevan Kansa Association was formed and he was elected president.

Late in the summer of 1899, 180 Finns left for Queensland, approximately half of them firmly committed to Kurikka and the Kalevan Kansa. The Australian government subsidized the emigrants' passage, and upon their arrival transported them either to the railway line being built to the mines, or to the cane fields in the north. Kurikka was offered 3000 marks to write a book in Finnish promoting the colony. In a letter to his daughter Aili he rejoiced: "Here there is complete liberty. No one asks for anyone's papers, and no one is asked where he comes from, only what he is capable of. There is complete freedom of religion and no censorship at all." He and fifty other Finns began work on the railway from Mareeba to Chillagoe.

It wasn't long, however, before the tone of Kurikka's letters changed. While the Australian government did provide some farm land for the Finns, they hoped to employ the majority of them to clear land for sugar plantations. Either way, there was no money to establish a utopian commune. On October 7, Kurikka wrote Aili, "We are being confronted with many difficulties. The Australians see the Finlanders as a source of cheap labour and a half-barbarous people."

In an attempt to raise money for his commune, Kurikka organized a contract to construct railway sleepers near Chillagoe in Queensland. After a couple of weeks the Finns felt that they were being cheated on their pay, and they held Kurikka, as leader, responsible. The men drifted off to other jobs, and Kurikka's utopia never got further than ten tents pitched near the railway line in Chillagoe. An Australian immigration agent later said, "Kurikka was an honest, well-meaning theorist and enthusiast, but as far as the utopia matter, a hopelessly impractical faddist."

Kurikka abandoned the railway sleepers and found a job in a factory making railway ties. The hard work and low wages were wearing, but worst of all, he was alone. It was at this point that Matti Halminen's letter arrived. Kurikka replied immediately. "I was lying exhausted in bed when your letter came," he wrote. "I have received two letters from Finland, both urging me to return to my homeland and accompanied by a promise to pay passage and expenses. As you know, I can no longer conceive of travelling to a Finland dominated by a Russian pirate government, except in the company of cannons and Mauser rifles. I am ready to leave Australia and to come to you. If you could send me travelling expenses, I would give myself solely to the founding of the commune. My hands are as calloused as anyone's and I'm prepared to do work of any kind. I want to be with you to plant the seed of betterment from which bountiful crops will grow for the joy of mankind and the glory of Finland."

In Nanaimo, the Finns scraped together the $125 fare and sent it to Kurikka.

CHAPTER FOUR

To Build a New Finland

Go forward people of Kalevala,
Away from the drudgery of wage work:
Your path goes toward freedom,
Servitude does not prosperity bring.
Whosoever shall embrace the present,
Shall stumble as before.
Whosoever for freedom yearns,
Can from us attain a sense of brotherhood.

Matti Kurikka 1901

K URIKKA ARRIVED IN NANAIMO IN THE FALL
of 1900. Along with his battered suitcase, he brought
with him nearly twenty years of experience in promoting socialism. Dedicated to the emancipation of the working class, his dream was to create an utopian society where Finns could live together in harmony, free from Russian oppression and the dictates of the church. Determined to make his utopia a reality, Kurikka spent his first weeks in Canada spreading his message in temperance halls. His confident and charismatic manner made a cooperative, communal effort seem practical as well as imaginative.

"In Finland I was popular as a writer," he told the Finns, "but what room is there in Finland for a man who has advanced ideas? Finns must either be dominated by Russia or leave the country. To have a home is the Utopia of a Finlander. Many will join us . . . to build a new Finland."

To raise funds for the utopian venture a joint stock company was formed, with five hundred shares valued at $200 each. The income generated by selling these shares was supposed to provide the company with operating capital. Many of the Finns did not have $200, so members were asked to make a down payment of $50 or, as a last resort, to pledge to pay for their shares with labour. As acting president, Kurikka suggested naming the company the Kalevan Kansa Colonization Company after his failed utopia in Australia.

Not having any cash to buy land, the Kalevan Kansa began investigating other options. In the spring of 1901 Halminen and Kurikka travelled to British Columbia's capital, Victoria, where they met with the chief commissioner of lands and works, and were given maps showing Crown land available on the coast. Halminen studied the maps and discovered that Malcolm Island seemed to have everything they were looking for. The island was removed from other settlements, yet appeared to be conveniently close to the shipping lanes. Although currently blanketed with timber, the 28,000 acres were designated as prime agricultural land for that part of the country.

Halminen told Kurikka and the Kalevan Kansa board of directors about his find and, without even visiting the island, they decided that it was the perfect site for their utopia. When they approached the government however, they learned that Malcolm Island was part of a 256,000-acre timber lease which had been given to the Industrial Power Company on June 6, 1901. The BC Legislature had recently passed an act allowing the government to lease pulp lands at an incredibly low price, and the Industrial Power Company was one of many companies hastily formed by former government officials and businessmen to take advantage of the situation. Determined to have Malcolm Island at any cost, the Finns began negotiating with the pulp company for a contract to log the timber.

While these arrangements were being made, Kurikka taught English to the Finns and lectured on the proposed utopia both locally and abroad. He explained that every aspect of the commune, from meals to child rearing, would be handled on a cooperative basis. Men and women would be employed at an equal wage, with meals and clothing supplied by the company and considered part of the pay. He said that members would require little in the way of money, as the company would look after most of their needs. The Kalevan Kansa would also take care of children, the sick and the elderly. Children would be admitted to the commune free of charge, with the understanding that when they were grown they would work for the colony and look after the older generation.

Everywhere he went Kurikka preached that "Bourgeois society is in a state of decay. We must show this rotting world the possibility of utopian society; we must create a model community founded on selfless regard for the well-being of others. Once this model is seen, people will abandon their present lives, and hasten to join us . . . to express the concept of utopia to the rest of the world." Kurikka had no doubt that other communities would follow their example, and that sooner or later "the whole nation will join us."

One Sunday, shortly after the site for the commune had been chosen, Halminen and some other Kalevan Kansa members went to August Oberg's home in Nanaimo where Kurikka was staying. Halminen later recalled: "When we arrived Kurikka was pensive and depressed, not at all his usual stimulating and lively self." Discouraged by the lengthy negotiations with the government and the pulp company, Kurikka admitted that he missed newspaper work and had accepted a job in Oregon working for the Finnish-American paper, the Liinnetar (Female Spirit of the West). His bags were packed and he planned to leave the next day.

Halminen expressed everyone's feelings when he said: "Now it seemed that our last hope for establishing a cooperative company had faded since without Kurikka's assistance we did not have the faith to make it happen. We needed his eloquence and sharp pen, for practical matters we could have depended on ourselves."

After a lengthy silence Halminen offered a solution. "Why go to Astoria? Let's establish a newspaper here so you can write about our utopian settlement."

Kurikka replied, "If you can organize a newspaper I will run it for only the price of my food."

Halminen talked to ten friends who agreed to purchase ten-dollar shares in the newspaper. The idea generated so much excitement that Halminen, accompanied by Kalle Hendrickson and Herman Baund, walked the twelve kilometres to Extension to sell more shares. At Extension they found most of the Finns at an evangelical meeting led by Finnish Lutheran pastor Johan Lundell. Additional shares for the newspaper were sold and the *Aika* (Time), the first printed Finnish-language newspaper in Canada, was formed. Prior to this, the only Finnish newspapers had been a few *nyrkkilehti* (fist papers), written by hand and distributed by temperance groups.

Printing equipment for the *Aika* was found in a church basement where it had been stored by the out-of-business Nanaimo Review. Even though the press required additional letters to print Finnish, Halminen and Kurikka purchased it for $600. The New York Amerikan Tyomies donated the necessary letters, but the old press was so slow and cumbersome that the first issues of the newspaper were printed at the *Nanaimo Free Press*.

The *Aika* made its debut on May 6, 1901, became a weekly on May 17, and soon had subscribers throughout Canada and the United States, as well as Finland and Australia. An office opened at 77 Prideaux Street in Nanaimo, where yearly subscriptions were sold for $1.50, with advertisements available at $1.00 per column inch with discounts for continuing accounts. In Finland, the Czar declared the newspaper subversive and issues were routinely confiscated by the secret police.

Kurikka, recalling the censorship when he was editor of the Tyomies, reveled in his new freedom. In his first editorial he predicted that British Columbia Finns "would show the way to freedom for the working class," and in an article titled "The Harmony Idea" he wrote, ". . . the only road to a better life lies in cooperation, love, and generosity. But this cannot be obtained immediately. It will be necessary to prove that mutual cooperation and action is possible, then attempt to get the surrounding disorder to organize." In the same vein he continued, "Do unto others what you wish them to do unto you. What prevents this? A society Lased on competition and internal strife. In addition to the economic teachings of socialism, we must learn to understand that there is but one great natural science . . . its invisible aspect is the great spirit which Jesus called "Our Father.""

Kurikka wrote to the provincial government asking it to formally announce its intention to grant land to the Finns and advising that he was advertising in North American and Finnish newspapers, as well as the newly formed *Aika*, for members to join the Kalevan Kansa. Headlines in the Vancouver *Province* read, "Russian Finns Seek Home," while the Victoria *Daily Colonist* predicted that, "This scheme could add 10,000 to the population of British Columbia." In an interview with one of the papers, Kurikka proudly but falsely boasted, "There is plenty of money behind the project."

Travelling and lecturing throughout Canada and the United States, Kurikka encouraged his listeners to, "Go forward you people of Kalevala, away from the drudgery of wage work. Your path points to freedom, servitude will not bring prosperity." He urged temperance and separation from the church, saying: "Alcoholism is hindering our ideals. The Church thinks drinking spirits is normal because man is naturally sinful but this is not so. Man longs to be good and is, it is traditional society which stops people from listening to their hearts. Harmony was present before priests became involved with Christianity and it can be present again."

Many of the Finns who heard Kurikka embraced his ideas wholeheartedly, but some were strong Lutherans and viewed him as the Anti-Christ. When Kurikka visited the Finnish-American Labor Lodge in New York, Lutheran priests told the police that a dangerous anarchist would be lecturing. The police raided the hall during Kurikka's speech, broke up the meeting and came close to causing a riot. In British Columbia, Lundell, a Lutheran pastor who had been preaching in Nanaimo since 1893, called Kurikka "the Devil incarnate who was leading the Finns to spiritual bankruptcy." Lundell warned his congregation to stay away from Kurikka and requested the government to prohibit the radical from speaking in public.

When Kurikka began to receive death threats for his attacks against the church, even he realized that he had gone too far. He asked the Kalevan Kansa to send for Austin Mäkelä, "his best and most trusted friend." Kurikka said he felt "like a fierce unmanageable train engineer who needed someone to act as brakeman when the velocity became too high." Kurikka trusted Mäkelä, a university friend and fellow newspaperman from Finland, to be such a brakeman. A collection was taken for travelling expenses and soon Mäkelä and his wife Elli were en route to Nanaimo.

Plans for the colony were receiving wide coverage in the English-language newspapers. The Daily Herald, Nanaimo's working-class newspaper, wrote, "The Finns are a group of people who promote industry, refinement, and a belief in realistic idealism." The newspaper criticized the government for not proceeding with the land grant, saying, "If the Finns wanted to exploit the natural resources, destroy the forests, and drain the mineral deposits, they would certainly have been made warmly welcome. But when they want to add to the land's prosperity, not impoverish it, they are pushed to the limit." The Victoria *Daily Colonist* referred to the Finns as an "industrious, frugal, and easily contented people willing to work hard to secure peaceful homes," while a letter to the editor praised, "Kurikka's proposal to employ immigrant Finns in the building of the railway from Victoria to upper Vancouver Island." Even Dunsmuir was quoted as saying that, "no white men in the area around Malcolm Island will suffer from the land grant."

By this time the Kalevan Kansa had negotiated a contract to log and bark 150,000 cords of timber for the Industrial Power Company. In the August 2, 1901, issue of the *Aika*, Kurikka wrote: "The course of the Kalevan Kansa has progressed slowly but surely. The legal papers have been prepared in English by attorneys Baker and Potts, who say that our agreement reads more like the founding principles of a constitution than the regulations of a company. We have received a favourable letter from the government and can see nothing that would prevent a positive decision." The article continued: "In the beginning, a limited amount of men will be sent to the island. This number will depend on how many are capable of purchasing a share. Those who wish to be in the first group should expect to pay a minimum of $50.00. No doubt there will be some who wish to underwrite the entire amount of their share through labour, but these members should be limited."

Kurikka further encouraged membership in his August 23 editorial. "Come here you proper sons and daughters of Finn mothers who comprehend that freedom is at the start and finish of man's purpose . . . Come here to live with us in freedom, where all are equal in the harmony of shared thoughts, and all find satisfaction and pleasure in the protection of the weak."

The Kalevan Kansa was formally registered as a company on November 8, 1901, with goals "to organize colonies and aid Finn and other immigrants in British Columbia, and to obtain land in British Columbia by purchase, pre-emption,

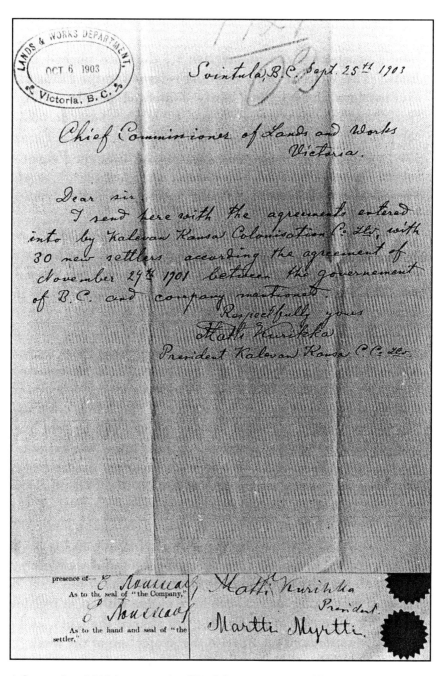

Lands & Works Department
OCT 6 1903
Victoria, B.C.

Sointula, B.C. Sept. 25th 1903

Chief Commissioner of Lands and Works
Victoria.

Dear sir,
    I send here with the agreements entered
into by Kalevan Kansa Colonisation Co. Ltd, with
30 new settlers according the agreement of
November 29th 1901 between the government
of B.C. and company mentioned.
                        Respectfully yours
                        Matti Kurikka
            President Kalevan Kansa C.C. Ltd.

presence of— E. Rouseau
    As to the seal of "the Company,"
    E. Rouseau
    As to the hand and seal of "the settler,"

Matti Kurikka
President.
Martti Myrtti.

A September 1903 letter to the Chief Commissioner of Lands and Works
from Matti Kurikka, President of the Kalevan Kansa. (Rick James;
BCARS GR140)

or other means, for the establishment of colonies which are to be governed by a program of common labour and mutual service." On November 29, the Finns and the Chief Commissioner of Lands and Works, W.C. Wells, acting on behalf of His Majesty King Edward VII of England, signed a formal agreement for Malcolm Island. Among other things the agreement stated that ownership of the island would be transferred to the Finns in seven years provided that 350 settlers (one for each eighty acres) had built homes on the island and made improvements to the amount of $2.50 per acre. The colonists were also required to become British subjects, educate their children in English and build their own wharves, bridges, roads and public buildings. If the Finns were successful, the government pledged to grant them additional property similar in size to Malcolm Island.

Kurikka celebrated the occasion by writing: "We have passed the steepest precipice. The Finns from Nanaimo and Extension have performed a deed which will be mentioned in the history of humanity. We now have an island rich in natural beauty, blessed with a good climate, and near prosperous shipping routes. There we will create our own country . . . bringing all Finns to live within its shelter."

Carried away by his vision, Kurikka continued, "Δ44

We will be self-sufficient and produce everything we need. Unemployment and sickness will evaporate into the past and strikes and poverty will become unknown. It only depends on us to break free from the feet of the capitalists and to become equals. Only then will the characteristics of our nationality have an opportunity to blossom and prosper!"

What the colony needed now was capital. While Kurikka was confident that eventually 2000 settlers from Finland and the United States would emigrate to Malcolm Island, he was afraid that a lack of funds would doom this utopia just as it had the original Kalevan Kansa in Australia. Desperate to entice members with money, he made a private arrangement

This Agreement made in duplicate this *Thirty first* day of *May*, A. D. 1902, between "THE KALEVAN KANSA COLONISATION COMPANY, LIMITED," hereinafter called "the Company," of the first part, and *Theodore Tanner* hereinafter called "the settler," of the second part:

WHEREAS by an agreement bearing date the 29th day of November, A. D. 1901, between His Majesty the King, represented by the Chief Commissioner of Lands and Works, for the Province of British Columbia, and the above-mentioned Company (a copy of which agreement is hereto annexed), the Company, upon complying with the terms of said agreement, has the right to acquire grant of Malcolm Island for the purpose of establishing upon said Island colonies or settlements of Finlanders and others;

AND WHEREAS the said settler desires to locate upon said Island, subject to the terms of said Agreement, and the Company have agreed to allow him to enjoy the privileges of resident shareholder of the Company, according to the Articles of Association of the Company:

NOW, THEREFORE, THIS AGREEMENT WITNESSETH that the settler, for himself, his heirs, executors, administrators and assigns, in consideration of being allowed by the Company to enjoy the privileges of resident shareholder of the Company, according to the Articles of Association of the Company, hereby covenants and agrees that he, his heirs, executors, administrators or assigns, shall not have any vested right in or to any land he may be allowed to occupy as such resident shareholder on account of improvements made, or to be made, by him or them, or settlement duties performed, or to be performed, by him or them upon said land, and shall not make any claim upon His Majesty the King or the Government of the Province of British Columbia for or in respect of said land or improvements.

The said settler hereby further covenants and agrees as follows:—

(a.) That, as soon as possible, he will take the oath of allegiance to His Majesty the King and his successors, and become a duly naturalized British subject;

(b.) That he will conform, in every respect, to the requirements of the law without reference to any conscience clauses or religious or political doctrines that he may hold:

(c.) That he will, whenever called upon, bear arms in defence of the country;

(d.) That all his children shall be educated in the public schools in the English language.

IN TESTIMONY WHEREOF "the Company" have hereunto affixed their corporate seal and "the settler" has hereunto set his hand and seal the day and year first above written.

Signed, sealed and delivered in the presence of—

As to the seal of "the Company," *10 H Halliday*

Matti Kurikka
President

As to the hand and seal of "the settler," *Theodore Tanner*

O H Halliday

The agreement between the Kalevan Kansa and Theodore Tanner signed in May 1902. (Rick James; BCARS GR140)

with James Dunsmuir. The coal mine owner agreed to hire up to 200 Finns on Kurikka's recommendation, at a daily wage of $2.50. Kurikka, of course, would only recommend men who agreed to join the Kalevan Kansa, and who also agreed to pay at least five dollars each month toward their membership fee. This plan would have put as much as $1000 per month into the company account and would have provided enough money for work to begin on the island.

The standard wage at that time was three dollars per day, however, and the thought of providing cheap labour for the man the mine workers called the "millionaire and skinner of men" was too much for the miners. In his first disagreement with the board of directors Kurikka pounded his fist on the table and argued that, "We have no responsibility toward those others, we are only responsible for the Kalevan Kansa!" To this the directors angrily replied, 'The Kalevan Kansa will not be founded by trampling the wages of others and turning them against us!"

In the meantime another group of miners was trying to organize a union and at a large meeting at the Nanaimo Opera House, people began to ask questions about this plan to enlist low-paid Finn workers. While the meeting was taking place, Dunsmuir, who had heard rumours about unionization, arrived in Nanaimo. When he found only a few men present at the South Wellington mine, he ripped a piece of paper from his pocket and wrote, "At this mine work shall be discontinued indefinitely." With one sentence Dunsmuir exerted his authority, and Kurikka's plan became worthless.

CHAPTER FIVE

Steady and Level Headed

Oh Malcolm Island, Sointula,
Our home of peace and happiness,
Why ever were you created?
That is only known to Him.
Of all that He has created on earth
You have been granted to us.
To us you are precious
For you give us peace.

Matti Kurikka 1902

WHILE MATTI KURIKKA WAS CLASSICALLY tall, dark and handsome, Austin Mäkelä possessed a lean frame topped by big ears and blonde hair that curled at the neck. Born in the same year as Kurikka, Mäkelä also attended the University of Helsinki but his studies were interrupted by the death of his father. Forced to give up his plans to become a lawyer, in 1887 Mäkelä went to work as an elementary school teacher. It was during this time that he met the intellectual activist Minna Canth and became a Marxist socialist.

After a few years Mäkelä gave up teaching to work with Kurikka on the Viipurin *Sanomat* and later the *Työmies*, where he eventually became editor. Steady and level-headed, Mäkelä focused on the issues at hand rather than his own opinions. As one reader said, Mäkelä was "much more dangerous to his opposition than the shifting and inconsistent Kurikka."

It was through his brother-in-law, the revolutionary Johan Kock, that Mäkelä began shipping subversive books in to Russia and organizing the smuggling of revolutionaries out. Following his Marxist leanings, he helped found the Labour Party of Finland, and in 1901 was chosen to be a member of the party's leading council. As soon as he received Kurikka's summons, however, he abandoned both the newspaper and his political activities. Some said that Mäkelä left Finland a little too quickly. There were hints that his drinking, "a weakness already apparent during his student years," according to Finnish historian Erkki Salomaa, had caused problems with the Labour Party and the *Työmies*, while others speculated that the

Russian secret police were investigating his involvement with the "northern railroad."

As soon as Mäkelä reached Nanaimo he was appointed acting

Finnish Marxist Austin Mäkelä, circa 1880s. In Canada Mäkelä was a journalist, justice of the peace and lighthouse keeper. After Kurikka left Sointula, Mäkelä became the guiding influence on the island. (Tanner collection)

secretary of the Kalevan Kansa and became joint editor of the *Aika*. Early in 1902, the board of directors sent Mäkelä to inspect Malcolm Island. He was not the first to visit the island, however. Late in 1901, after commercial fishing dosed for the season, Johan Mikkelson and Theodore Tanner had sailed from the Fraser River to Nanaimo in Mikkelson's five-and-a-half metre (eighteen foot) sailboat, the *Aino*. When they heard about the Finns' plans for an utopian commune, they volunteered to take a work crew to the island.

At dawn on December 6, 1901, Mikkelson and Tanner, accompanied by Kalle Hendrickson, Otto Ross, and Malakias Kytomma, began their 290-kilometre (180-mile) journey. Tanner, a well-read man with an interest in horticulture, wrote: "After all sorts of preparations we finally pulled the white sail-cloths up and began to speed towards the promised land. The morning was completely calm and we stuck to our oars, committed to reach our destination even if we had to row the entire way." An afternoon tailwind bellied their sails, skimming the small craft more than sixty-four kilometres (forty miles) until they anchored near a small island at dusk. During the night the wind increased, and by morning they had lost their anchor. They tied the *Aino* to a tree while they fashioned a crude replacement from a waterlogged piece of driftwood from the beach. Over the next few days, depending on the wind, they rowed and sailed their way up the coast.

Another entry in Tanner's journal reads: "Having reached the much feared Seymour Narrows, we waited for six hours until it was quiet enough for us to pass through. Shortly afterwards, Mikkelson noticed that a shotgun had been left on the cabin roof. When he picked it up it fired, ripping the veins and sinew of his right wrist."

While Tanner bandaged Mikkelson's arm and made him as comfortable as possible, the others rowed steadily, hoping to find a hospital somewhere in the sea and forest that surrounded them. With Mikkelson in pain and shock, the trip seemed endless, but on December 15 they found a physician at the village of Alert Bay on Cormorant Island. The doctor warned the Finns that Mikkelson's injury was serious and that he would probably lose his arm. Along with this dreary news they also learned that they were less than six kilometres (four miles) from their goal. They climbed back into the *Aino* and reached Malcolm Island just before dark.

In the morning they explored the coarsely gravelled beach, which was covered with an immense pile of driftwood. A thick forest of cedar, spruce and hemlock sloped upwards to a gently rolling plateau. Among a tangle of salal and berry bushes they found remnants of Spencer's commune, a rough wooden shack, and nearby on the beach, the remains of a steam plant and a pile of rusted pipes. They cleared brambles and hung tarps to replace the cabin's missing door and window, and arranged their blankets and gear on the floor.

During the night a south wind swept down the Nimp-kish Valley on Vancouver Island, crossing Broughton Strait to batter the bay where the Finns slept. The tarps snapped and tore at the door and window and trees crashed to the ground. When a flying branch skidded across the roof, the men bolted for the beach and the scanty shelter of the steam boiler to wait out the storm.

By the time Mäkelä reached the island in January 1902, the four men had repaired the shack and explored their new home. Heavy timber with low-growing branches, dense thickets of salal, and three metre (ten feet) high berry bush-es made access to the heart of the island difficult, but they showed Mäkelä Mitchell Bay on the southeast side of the is-land, and the deep indentation of Rough Bay near the centre of the south shore where they had landed. Mäkelä particularly liked Rough Bay, with its smooth, sandy bottom and the small stream that emptied into it.

In the next issue of the *Aika*, Mäkelä reported that Mal-colm Island contained arable land covered by abundant forests and surrounded by a bountiful sea. He recommended naming the utopia *Kotiksi* (Home Place) since the word *koti* (home) would continually remind members that they belonged to one family. "It will require a great deal of hard work to convert Malcolm Island to farm land," he wrote. "In the beginning settlers must be earnest, zealous, and prepared to do without luxuries. But later, when we have our own shipping and mail service, a school, store, meeting halls, and homes for everyone complete with gardens and livestock, what else could we need? Capability, enthusiasm, and endurance is all!"

Later, in his memoirs, Mäkelä confided, "In my opinion the island was very suitable as a place of refuge . . . for persecuted socialists in Finland. There would have been room for the whole Finnish working class. I thought of building a big ocean vessel which could bring the whole Finnish nation to that free land."

Mäkelä's glowing testimonials, plus others written by Kurikka, resulted in a surge of people eager to join the commune. The first to reach Nanaimo were two wood plant workers and a book binder from Finland, three shoemakers from Chicago, and newlyweds Andrew and Anna Wilander from New York. The directors had already sent Victor Saarikoski and Heikki Kilpeläinen, an experienced carpenter, to the island to build a cabin out of cedar logs. Now they obtained a loan to purchase a sailboat, the *Kalevatar* (Kaleva Queen), and five tons of food and other supplies. Arriving just in time for the trip were Kalle Hoffren from Washington State and Johan Malm from Australia. As no one in the group was familiar with sails, Hoffren, who had served in the American Navy, was placed in charge of the vessel. The trip was nearly a disaster. On more than one occasion the enthusiastic but inexperienced crew came close to capsizing the *Kalevatar*, and by the time they reached Malcolm Island they had lost the mast and sails.

Matti Halminen and J.E. Jerrman were the next to

arrive on the island. They found their fellow utopians hoeing a field that had been cleared by Spencer's group but was now overgrown with saplings. With fifteen people living on the island, the Spencer shack was crowded. Most of the men slept in a makeshift sauna, but no one complained, as they all agreed with Halminen who claimed that, "harmony creates space of its own." During the day Anna Wilander and Victor Saarikoski, looked after the meals while the others cleared fields, burned stumps and cut boards with an old country cleave saw.

A trail was blazed from the base of Rough Bay to the other side of the island, and one morning Halminen, Jerrman, and Vihtori Jalo hiked to the north shore and from there attempted to hack through the dense brush to the centre of the island. The most difficult part of the expedition was making it past the salal and berry bushes that skirted the shore. Once they penetrated this barrier, they found themselves in a dark forest with tall trees and sparse undergrowth. They discovered a brook with an old cabin at its mouth and a large marsh. Plans were made to build a trail to the marsh, drain it and plant vegetables and hay. Halminen, a ditch digger by trade, offered to be in charge of the operation.

By late spring the Kalevan Kansa had eighty-one members, with twenty living and working on the island. When Katri Riksman and Mrs. Salmi joined their husbands, the island's female population rose to three. For twenty-two-year-old Katri, Malcolm Island was the end of a journey that had begun in Finland. She and her husband Matti and their two children were living in Oregon when they heard a speech by Kurikka and decided to join the commune. "We arrived on the island late at night," she said. "It was pitch black out and the bay was covered with kelp that looked like big snakes in the water. The boat tied up to a slip and we had to walk along logs to the shore where a little cabin was. Inside there were five double bunks with hay for mattresses. Our family got one of the bunks."

Towards the end of May Kurikka headed for the island,

„KALEVAN KANSA COLONISATION COMPANY'n, LIMITED", PERUSSÄÄNNÖT.

———o———

1:si. Yhtiön nimi tulee olemaan „Kalevan Kansa, Colonisation Company, Limited."

2:si. Yhtiön rekisteröity virasto sijaitsee vastaiseksi Nanaimossa.

3:si. Tarkoitukset, mitä varten yhtiö on muodostettu, ovat:—

(a.) Suomalaisten ja muitten siirtymisen auttaminen ja siirtolain eli kotikontujen järjestäminen British Columbiaan.

(b.) Hankkia ostamalla, pre-emptionilla tahi muilla keinoin maata sanotun maakunnan sisällä, joihin rakentaa siirtoloita Suomalaisille ja muille, ja tullen nämä siirtolat hallittaviksi keskinäistä yhteistyötä ja avuliaisuutta tarkoittavan ohjelman mukaan.

(c.) Järjestää ja ylläpitää niissä siirtoloissa eli niillä kotikonnuilla kaikkia sellaisia ammattitöitä, teollisuuslaitoksia ja toimia, mitkä tarpeellisiksi nähdään sanottujen siirtolain jäsenien työnsaantia varten, ja hankkia heille oikean toimeentuloon tarvittavia elämäntarpeita.

(d.) Tehdä sopimuksia muitten yhtiöitten eli henkilöitten kanssa tarveaineitten eli valmistettujen tavarain hankinnasta, taikka työn teosta sellaisille yhtiöille eli henkilöille.

(e.) Ostaa, myydä, vuokrata eli arenteerata maita tahi kaivoksia ja viljellä, kehittää ja pitää niitä käytännössä.

(f.) Harjoittaa maanviljelystä, kalastusta, sahaliikettä, teollisuutta ja kauppaa.

(g.) Laittaa ja rakentaa teitä, laivasiltoja, tehtaita, sahoja, höyryveneitä, laivoja ja tehdä muita sellaisia asioita, jotka helpottavat ja edistävät ylläsanottuja tarkoituksia.

(h.) Ostaa muitten yhtiöitten taikka henkilöitten yrityksiä.

(i.) Sulautua yhteen jonkun muun yhtiön tahi muitten yhtiöitten kanssa, joilla on sama tahi samanlainen tarkoitus.

4:si. Jäsenien vastuunalaisuus on rajoitettu.

5:si. Yhtiön pääoma on sata tuhatta dollaria ($100,000), jaettu viiteen sataan 200 dollarin osakkeeseen.

Certified a correct translation

Nanaimo, B. C. June 10th 1902

Matti Kurikka

Witness.
Austin McKela

A translation of the Kalevan Kansa agreement signed by Matti Kurikka, 1902. (Rick James; BCARS GR140)

taking with him $500 worth of supplies purchased on credit and the colony's first physician, Dr. Oswald Beckman. Easily recognized by his booming voice and imposing 106-kilogram (235-pound) bulk, Beckman had emigrated from Finland to the United States as a young man and found work as a hospital orderly. When the hospital board realized that he was fluent in seven languages, it offered to sponsor a medical education. In the meantime, his robust voice had earned him an invitation to study opera in Italy. A practical man, Beckman chose to become a doctor. He and his second wife were operating a private hospital in Astoria when Kurikka convinced them to join the Kalevan Kansa.

A few days into June, word reached Malcolm Island that a large group was coming to celebrate Juhannus (Mid Summer's Eve). Working feverishly, the men constructed a speaker's platform on a large cedar stump, finished the cedar cabin and purchased a slaughter cow from William May, one of the first settlers on northern Vancouver Island. The Kalevan Kansa rented the Coquitlam to transport people from Nanaimo to the island. When the steamship departed it was crammed with men, women and children, as well as a sawmill, farming equipment and other miscellaneous supplies. The Coquitlam unloaded its passengers and cargo on June 21, 1902, and the Juhannus festivities began. Passionate and stirring poems, songs and speeches were delivered from the speaker's podium by Kurikka, Mäkelä, Beckman and Martin Hendrickson, a former temperance advocate turned socialist. Their words created a vivid image of a society free from the adverse affects of police, alcohol and the church, where each person would work for the common good.

The speeches excited everyone, especially the women.

Katri said: "They emphasized that women would be equal with men. At that time women had no property, voting or wage rights whatsoever. On Malcolm Island we would receive the same wages as men, would have the right to speak at meetings and to vote. And we had to work, everyone had to work."

Kurikka and Mäkelä presented the Kalevan Kansa's first annual report. The colony now numbered 127 adults with cash in hand totalling $324 and an outstanding debt of $1300, plus wages due to members. In addition to money from membership shares, the company had been given $114.45, $100 of which was used to start a piano fund while the remainder was earmarked for immigration assistance.

Mäkelä outlined plans for an idyllic village on the east shore of Rough Bay, complete with treed streets, parks, beach promenades, public buildings and workshops. A large strip along the shoreline would be set aside as a market place and the minimum size for a building lot would be half an acre. He noted that, "without substantial private capital or large loans, we have gotten off to a good start with a momentum that couldn't be better."

A lot of time was spent discussing ways to organize labour. While the colonists wished to encourage efficiency, they also wanted to foster a sense of independence and individual responsibility. It was decided to form work groups which would select their own leaders. These leaders, together with an elected project organizer, would assign tasks. It was agreed that each adult would receive a wage of a dollar a day, plus food, lodging and clothing. An eight-hour shift would be standard, while those performing more strenuous jobs would work fewer hours. At the end of the fiscal year each person would receive a five percent dividend on their stock in the company, half of which would he put into a common account for recreation, cultural pursuits and other benefits.

A board of twelve directors was elected with August Oberg as treasurer and project organizer, Mäkelä as secretary, and Beckman as vice-president and manager. While the vice-president, secretary, treasurer and manager were appointed by the board, the president was elected by a majority of the colonists. The vote for Kurikka was unanimous.

After three days and nights of celebrating, exploring and bonfires on the beach, the settlers gathered to name the site of their utopia. Sointula (Harmony) was chosen over Mäkelä's previous suggestion of *Kotiksi*. Beckman proposed a colony flag featuring a white outline of Malcolm Island on a blue background. On the island would appear a golden *kantele*, a small harp that holds a prominent place in the *Kalevala* and is a symbol of Finnish culture.

Inspired by the idea of Sointula, all who had come north on the *Coquitlam* spontaneously decided to remain. Since the two cabins were already full, tents were ordered to house the overflow. As the island had no post office, Mäkelä agreed to return to Nanaimo where he would run the *Aika* and process membership applications. The future seemed bright for the colonists; there was wood to build with, berries to eat and song birds everywhere. Halminen wrote later, "Everyone worked so hard, with this group it truly seemed possible that we could build a utopia."

Shoemakers and Tailors

THROUGHOUT THE SUMMER OF 1902, A STEADY banging of hammers measured the progress on a storage shed and a communal kitchen and dining room. Each afternoon, a westerly breeze lifted the morning blanket of fog to reveal a couple of pens with some chickens and a few pigs and a field of blossoming potato plants. Two milk cows wandered in and out of the woods, and on the other side of the island Matti Halminen ditched the marsh, planted more potatoes and built a small cabin and a shed for meadow grass.

Johan Mikkelson, minus a thumb from his accident onboard the *Aino*, had finally reached the island and was now in charge of food fishing. Salmon and halibut were abundant, and it wasn't long before every barrel and container was filled with fillets layered with a thick crust of rock salt. Hunting crews kept the colony supplied with venison and grouse, while berry pickers gathered bushels of salal berries which were crushed into a tart, purple juice or poured over rice and called dessert. A makeshift factory was producing bricks from clay found near the Spencer shack. The Vancouver *Province* reported, "Although unfinished and crude, Sointula manufactures a brick that is nearly as heavy and hard as the best on the market."

A shelter had been raised around the smithy and foundry, where a couple of men created forms and melted iron to

Sointula settlers, 1902. (SM)

make machinery parts. "They had three or four big ovens to melt the iron," recalled Richard Michelson. "There wasn't any coke around so they made their own charcoal out of wood. It was quite a job, a watchman had to be there night and day. There was one man, a tailor by trade, who didn't like watching the charcoal, but everyone had to do whatever was necessary."

Late that summer, timber cruiser and prospector West Huson informed the Vancouver *Province* that, "the Finns in Sointula bought stone from my quarry on Haddington Island to build chimneys and a boiler. You never saw such hard workers—in five years they'll run the whole country up there. Why they even eat raw fish—I've seem them eat a piece of bread with a slice of raw salmon on it for lunch!"

The Finns took a break from all their hard work on Saturday and Sunday. Once a week's worth of grime was removed in the sauna, the sound of an accordion, trumpet or mouth organ was enough to rejuvenate even the weariest of bodies. Saturday nights were filled with music, dancing, plays and debates. Everyone was encouraged to participate, and the lively, often heated debates were looked forward to every bit as much as the plays and dances. Social activities took place outside during good weather, otherwise everyone crowded into the dining hall.

On Sundays Katri Riksman ran the "library," a collection of 2000 Finnish language books that had been donated by a Finnish organization in Australia. Although lack of space meant that many of the books stayed in their shipping cartons, Katri managed to convert the dining area into a reading room for at least a few hours each week. Sunday was also the day that Kurikka taught English, lectured and read literary works aloud. Even without any formal religion, there was a great deal of interest in spiritual matters. As Matti Halminen said, "We discussed spiritual issues thoroughly, everyone was interested, especially when Kurikka and Mäkelä took opposite sides during a debate."

Although Kurikka was against the church he felt that some sort of spiritual order was necessary. To him, theosophy, with its emphasis on love, truth, freedom and harmony with nature, made sense. Kurikka told the colonists that, "The fulfillment of our Father's will does not consist in sighing, suffering, and swallowing his flesh and blood on Sunday." Instead he encouraged them to "worship God seven days a week instead of one" and to "seek spiritual harmony in music, literature, drama, and artistic workmanship."

Mäkelä, on the other hand, rejected theosophy as "the seventeenth form of religion that they have tried to force upon me in my lifetime," and said that it was nothing better than "an attempt to dress up ancient religious fantasies in modern looking dress."

Occasionally religious leaders came to the island, but the Finns were unfriendly and discouraged contact. One evangelist insisted on staying in Sointula but soon gave up trying to convert the islanders and left. Mäkelä, who had a reputation as a humorous writer, wrote a play based on this visit. In Mäkelä's skit, the clergyman was so impressed with Sointula and what it stood for that he gave up religion to join the Kalevan Kansa.

Being away from the *Aika* did not prevent Kurikka from churning out articles for the newspaper. While his goal was to recruit members with capital, the majority of his writing stressed the need for idealism rather than cash. A typical issue advised newcomers to "Bring your entire effects—all is needed here," then went on to say, "people are needed who are congenial, unselfish, devoted, and willing to sacrifice much. If you are uncertain of your strength of character, or suspect human goodness and nobleness, you would do well to stay away."

A steady flow of predominantly young people responded to the challenge and while many did bring all their possessions, few had any money to pay for a membership. Mäkelä said: "Often without warning, people streamed into the colony—single men, families with children. They came from hundreds, thousands of miles away, many directly from Finland. What could one do except bid them welcome, and accept them as members, whether there was accommodation or not?"

A willingness to work was evident (as soon as Mrs. Neuvo set foot on the island she marched to the kitchen, demanded a knife and began to peel potatoes), but most of the newcomers were artisans and professionals who were unsuited for, and largely ignorant of the tasks they were asked to perform. To make the most of members' skills, and in an effort to make the community self-sufficient, the Kalevan Kansa ordered supplies for its craftspeople on credit. Leather shoes and finely stitched suits were advertised in the *Aika*, but it soon became obvious that these items cost more money than they made. By the time raw materials were shipped in and the finished product shipped out, merchandise made in Sointula was far more expensive than the ready-made item. Also, although Malcolm Island was close to coastal shipping lanes, its docking facilities were only suitable for small boats, and the nearest port of any size was Cormorant Island, a six-kilometre (four-mile) row away.

Providing milk for all the young families on the island was far beyond the capabilities of the two free-range milk cows. Funds had been set aside for a piano, but Mäkelä insisted that this money be used to purchase dairy cows. Kurikka argued against the idea as he "longed for some spiritual food, music in Sointula," but Mäkelä forced him to face the reality of the situation. Early in the fall Kurikka, Mäkelä, and Halminen bought eleven dairy cows and a five-year-old Durham bull in Nanaimo. Forty people joined the herd for its trip north, prompting Halminen to call the *Capilano* "a little Noah's ark filled with men, women, children, cattle, hens, and dogs, all bound for Sointula." The voyage ended in a downpour, and in the slanting wetness tents were pitched and the cattle let loose to fend for themselves.

The Kalevan Kansa now had milk cows but didn't have any way to feed them. Work parties were forced to travel as far away as Kingcome and Knight inlets to cut grass on the river flats. Eventually the cattle were moved to Vancouver Island and kept in some abandoned buildings that had a bit of cleared land around them. This meant that several men had to stay with the cows, while others kept busy ferrying feed to the animals and milk to the colonists.

Since all the members of the Kalevan Kansa were now living on Malcolm Island, it was decided to move the *Aika* there as well. The last Nanaimo issue of the newspaper appeared on

September 2, 1902, but with no place to set the press up in Sointula, production did not resume until November, 1903. For much of his time in Canada, Kurikka had belittled Finnish-American newspapers for their "class minded socialism," and accused them of promoting materialism and conflict. Now, even though he was a popular and imaginative writer, many Finnish newspapers refused to publish his work.

By November there were over 200 people living on the island. The wind had shifted to the southeast, bringing with it gray skies and a persistent bone-chilling rain. Life was cold, wet and miserable, especially for those sleeping in tents. With winter upon them, work began on what was to be the first of many communal houses. The three-story building was completed in a few weeks, with the top floor designated as a meeting room and temporary tailor's shop, and the two lower floors divided by 66-metre (72-feet) long hallways and partitioned into twenty-eight sleeping rooms. On the first floor, next to the door, was Kurikka's office and sleeping quarters, with a large mortar baking oven at the other end of the hallway. Flues— some metal and some wood—extended from the oven throughout the building to provide heat to the rooms. Green lumber had been used and the boards soon shrank, leaving large cracks in the walls and floors. Sounds slipped easily through these crevices and the communal house was soon nicknamed Melula (Noisy).

Melula came too late for some. Used to comfortable surroundings and a steady income, they had not fully understood the philosophy of the colony and the conditions under which they would be living. The continual rain, a dreary overcast sky and the lack of conveniences prompted some members to leave. Frustrated that they had nothing to show for their investment of time and money, a few wrote to newspapers complaining about the Kalevan Kansa. Among them was Martin Hendrickson, a former agitator on the socialist speaking circuit. When Hendrickson had visited Sointula to speak at Juhannus, he had been so impressed that he had joined the colony and quickly became one of Kurikka's closest friends and admirers. However, it wasn't long before Hendrickson, a staunch Marxist, was criticizing the commune and arguing with Kurikka. Eventually he left the island, disillusioned both with Kurikka and his utopian socialism.

Even as Hendrickson and others were leaving, new members were arriving. Kurikka had spread the word about Sointula widely, if somewhat inaccurately. The *Aika* had described Sointula as a thriving communal colony, when the reality was a heavily forested island being labouriously cleared by hand. Under the impression that the island was fertile farm land, five wealthy families from the Dakotas travelled north in a caravan of wagons, plows and livestock. John and Ida Tynjala's wagon held five children, while Herman and Maria Hantula brought six children, as well as Kurikka's longed-for piano. Seven horses also made the journey and although five of the animals were left in Vancouver, the presence of Julious and Jumbo again brought up the subject of a barn.

One of the Dakota families donated money to buy a boat and a seine net for fishing, and in an effort to resolve the livestock problem a crew loaded the *Vinetta* with lumber and set off to build a barn at Wakeman Sound, ninety-six kilometres (sixty miles) away. The grassy plain that appeared to be an ideal pasture proved to be a tidal flat that was under two metres (six feet) of water twice a day. Hoping that they would find a better spot nearby, the men left the lumber under a tree, even though it could have been used in Sointula. When they went to retrieve the wood later, most of the planks were gone.

Earlier in the year a steam engineer named Hoikka and Lingren Nygren, one of the blacksmiths, had built a donkey engine out of an old boiler and winch salvaged from a steamship. This machine was used to haul logs at Mitchell Bay. Arvo Tynjala was six years old when his family left the Dakotas. "All the kids played in the woods, we had a game to see who could find the biggest tree. Once I found a cedar near where they were logging that was four and a half metres (fifteen feet) in diameter. The loggers had one of the horses pulling a line into the woods, then that steam donkey, a little bit of a coffee pot really, would pull the logs out. They didn't have a skid road, they just pulled them over the ground." A group of shoe-makers and tailors made up the logging crew, with a couple of young boys acting as whistle punks. Everyone joked that Sointula was the only place in the world where tailors knew more about logging than loggers, but it was no laughing matter when the size of the timber, the underpowered donkey and the enthusiastic but inept workers rendered the majority of the logs worthless before they even left the forest.

Originally, the colonists intended to sell the logs to the Industrial Power Company (they later realized that their con-tract had been little better than an agreement for slave labour), but a change of administration in the provincial government had resulted in the cancellation of the pulp lease. The Kal-evan Kansa's arrangement with the government could not be revoked because it had been made between the colonists and the King of England. This development meant that the Finns had the rights to all the timber on Malcolm Island. Initially, this sounded like good news, but the colonists soon realized that they were responsible for marketing and transporting the wood as well as cutting it. Since Kurikka had obtained loans for all supplies, including food, based on the Kalevan Kansa's contract with the Industrial Power Company, it was critical for the colony to generate some income.

Blessed with an endless supply of timber, the Finns de-cided to build a sawmill and sell processed lumber as well as logs. Although the colony had collected enough equipment for a sawmill and possessed many members who had worked in mills, no one had ever built one before. Determined, if not knowledgeable, they spent many frustrating weeks building the mill by trial and error. In the end, even the completion of the project was no cause for celebration. The makeshift mill cut lumber, but at a very slow rate.

By late winter, the entire colony was existing on credit. As president it was Kurikka's responsibility to obtain operating capital, and he often complained about how difficult this was, admitting that he frequently stretched the truth. The Kalevan Kansa had recently sold a log boom for $2000, receiving a $1000 down payment, but the boom was reported missing and presumed stolen in mid-December. In spite of this setback, Kurikka informed the press that "the colony was flourishing—100 are working in the new sawmill, with orders ahead for one year. They can turn out 150,000 board feet a day. It's likely that 2000 men, women, and children, from Finland and the eastern states will join us on Malcolm Island next summer."

On New Year's Day, 1903, the Vancouver *Province* reported, "Kurikka has interested United States capitalists in the Kalevan Kansa and they may come to BC to invest money in the enterprise." Near the end of January, however, the financial situation was so desperate that Kurikka went to Vancouver and placed advertisements in the newspaper asking for money to keep the Kalevan Kansa alive. Their suspicions aroused, the colony's creditors sent J. Warren Bell back to Malcolm Island with Kurikka. Bell's job was to assess the colony's assets before any further loans were granted.

In Sointula, Kurikka found that salvation had come from within. One member gave the company the $2000 he received from selling his property in North Dakota. In addition to this windfall, the colony's second log boom had reached Vancouver, the sawmill's steam engine had been repaired, and a track had been built to move materials between the sawmill and the storage site. Kurikka believed that the colony would be financially stable within one month. In another letter to Aili he said, "We continue to live in peace, eat at the same table and face hardships together. The colonists remain hopeful and contented."

Slander and Dark Speculations

A
S USUAL, WHEN KURIKKA RETURNED FROM Vancouver the colonists met to discuss business. It was January 29 when they gathered on the third floor of Melula. In light of recent events, some were opposed to obtaining further credit and a lively discussion took place. A tailor was the first to smell the smoke. It was just after 8:00 p.m. when his shout of "Fire!" halted the meeting. Kurikka quickly ordered everyone to follow him out of the building, while Mäkelä urged people to form an orderly line at the head of the stairs. In addition to the fifty-three people present at the meeting, eighty-four others, predominantly women and children, were in the sleeping rooms below. When Kurikka reached the ground floor and opened the door to the hall, he was forced back by a great blast of dense, hot smoke. Coughing and sputtering, he pushed his way outside, men, women and children flowing down the long stairway behind him. Smoke billowed from the rear of the ground floor hall, and the thin board partitions erupted in flame.

"By the time I got outside men and women were throwing children out of the second story windows and jumping after them," Kurikka later told the Vancouver *Province*. Bell, who had been resting in Kurikka's room on the ground floor, said: "The fire was the quickest I ever saw. I stood outside catching children as they were dropped from windows. The smoke and flames seemed to burst from every opening at once making it almost impossible to enter the hall. People leaped headlong through the windows, many of the women with their clothing and hair on fire."

Katri Riksman was still awake when she heard someone yell, "Fire!" "I jumped out of bed to see what I could save, then realized that I could only take the children. I took one under each arm and started for the lower level." The hall was dark and full of smoke and Katri could hear doors opening and shutting as other women, terrified by the smoke and screams, retreated back into their rooms. "Many jumped out of windows rather than pass the kerosene barrel stored by the front door but I just kept going." In the meantime her husband Matti had escaped from the third floor only to re-enter Melula in a frantic search for his family. Heat and smoke forced him to jump from a second-floor window.

On the same floor, engineer Isaac Heinonen panicked. He grabbed his buddy, a bricklayer named Arett Wallin, and begged him not to leave without him. Unfortunately, Heinonen's desperate grip prevented either man from moving. The two men swayed in the smoke, Wallin struggling to escape and Heinonen struggling to hang on. Those on the ground watched the drama through the second story windows where first it appeared that Wallin was in control, then it seemed that Heinonen was. Some thought that Wallin, known for possessing the strength of an ox, would conquer Heinonen, others thought that both men would die. "Finally," Kurikka said later, "after what seemed an age, and just when the flames were licking their way through the open window, Wallin raised the thoroughly insane engineer to the sill, and a moment later both men tumbled to the ground."

Mrs. Oberg was in one of the sleeping rooms on the ground floor when the fire broke out. She carried her two young sons outside, then found it impossible to return for her daughters. When her husband escaped from the third floor and heard that the girls were still inside, he plunged back into the flames. Finding the little girls huddled in bed, he picked them up and started for the door. Halfway there the floor collapsed. Oberg fell, Elma and Hilma slipping from his arms. With his clothes, face, and hands on fire, Oberg struggled to the door where he was pulled out by several men. The bodies of the girls were later found a few steps from the door.

Within minutes of the tailor's shout the interior of Melula was red with flame and filled with a heat so intense that it blistered the skin from a distance of four and a half metres (fifteen feet). Women and children on the ground floor were cut off from the outside door. A few of the rooms had no windows, while others had openings too small to even push a child through. Maria Hantula, a recent emigrant from the Dakotas, rescued two of her children and returned for the remaining four. She was found dead, crouched over her three children with the baby in her arms. Ann Lofbacka, a widow who had recently moved to Sointula from Extension, and her two children, Tekla and Oiva, died in a similar manner.

In one hour Melula was totally destroyed. The duplex that housed the Beckman family and their friends from Astoria, August and Marie Thompson, became the headquarters for the injured. Throughout the night the Finns carried countless pails of water from the ocean in an effort to save the duplex which was barely nine metres (thirty feet) from the inferno of Melula.

As an outsider, Bell was impressed by the courage of the Finns. "They were remarkable. One fellow had come out of a window like a catapult and landed face first. He tore the flesh off one side of his face and his hair was burned, yet he pulled himself together and carried water to fight the fire all night long."

Morning dawned on a grim site. There had been 137 people in the building which was now a smoking ruin. The critically injured included the blacksmith Nygren, who in addition to being burned had injured his back jumping from the third

Gravestone in memory of the eleven lives lost in the fire of January 29, 1903. 1990. (Rick James)

floor; Austin Mäkelä, who was badly burned on the face and hands and possibly blind; and Mrs. Neuvo, who had jumped from the second story and landed on her head. A score of others also suffered serious burns and bruises. In the ashes lay eleven bodies—one man, two women and eight children. The dead included Maria Hantula and her four children; Mrs. Lofbacka and her two children; the two Oberg girls; and Victor Sortell, an elderly blacksmith.

Bell told the Vancouver *Province*: "Looming up through the blackened debris were the remains of the stoves, iron bedsteads, and the metal portions of sewing machines. We tried to find out how many were lost, and the number grew from five to eleven. To add to the discomfort a high wind was blowing and with it came sleet and rain. Under an iron bedstead I found a human skull, and a few feet away, a baby's body all shrivelled up. A woman came up just as I was trying to get the body. I asked her if she had lost anyone in the fire. She murmured something about not understanding English, and then with a wail in her voice that I will never forget said, 'Baby, baby,' and pointed to the steaming ruins. I could not do or say anything. She put her apron to her eyes and a moment later was gone."

In addition to the dead and injured, personal papers, passports and thirteen tons of supplies stored in Melula were destroyed, and many of the colony's documents—including the company ledger and census lists—also went up in smoke. Those who had lived in the building were now homeless, and many of the women and children had only their night clothes to wear.

From the other side of the island, Halminen had noticed the sky over Sointula glowing red on the night of January 29. Early the next morning he set out to investigate. "Upon reaching Sointula," he said, "my heart beat so hard that I could feel it through my clothing. I could see that the communal house was missing and cannot describe the effect of that blow. The

Jury's report on the cause of the January 1903 fire that claimed eleven
lives as well as many of the Kalevan Kansa's records and supplies. (Rick
James; BCARS GR429)

strength went out of my feet and I lurched and slumped to the ground. To think that eleven people who were like brothers and sisters to me had been killed! After a few moments I went to the site of the fire where the bodies, some of which were just remains, were stretched out."

Two days later, relief in the way of bedding and food began to arrive from Alert Bay, and Kurikka and Bell travelled to Vancouver on the *Coquitlam* to seek further assistance. Kurikka informed the Vancouver *Province*, "While the colonists are adverse to receiving charity, many of the women and children are in urgent need of clothing. Most of the food was burned and there is no money to buy more."

The *Province* reported: "The fire left sixteen women, fourteen men, and forty-seven children totally destitute. Many of those escaped in their night clothes and are now living in tents. This evening the *Cassiar* leaves for the island and will carry free of charge any goods to help these people. They especially need clothing, underwear, boots, and shoes."

In addition to donations of clothes, food and money, the *Cassiar* also carried brandy and lint bandages for the injured, as well as two nurses who had volunteered to help Dr. Beckman. Those unpacking the supplies in Sointula were touched to find notes of sympathy tucked in among the items. The Sointula Relief committee voted to give all cash donations to the Kalevan Kansa to "at the earliest possible date build and furnish a hospital in Sointula which would be open and free for people from nearby areas as well as members of the commune."

On February 24, constable Walter Wollacott from Alert Bay reported to the attorney general that the bedding and clothing donated by the government and members of the public had made the settlers as comfortable as possible. He added that the colony especially needed sewing machines—as fifteen had been destroyed in the fire—and straw mattresses, since many of the colonists were now sleeping on the ground.

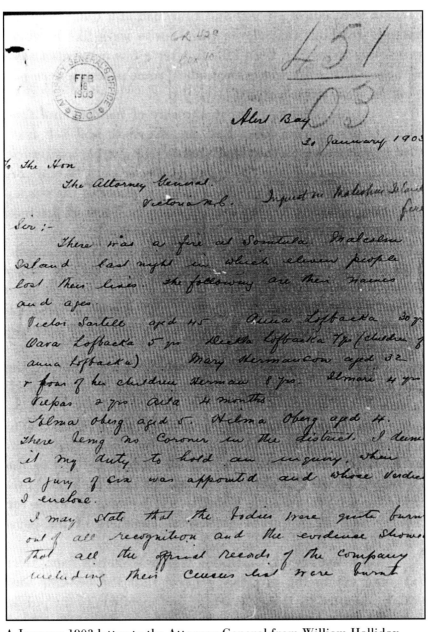

A January 1903 letter to the Attorney General from William Halliday about the fire on Malcolm Island. (Rick James; BCARS 451/03)

Second page of opposite.

As there was no coroner in the area, Alert Bay Justice of the Peace William Halliday formed a jury of six men to investigate the fire. Their verdict stated "that the parties came to their death by fire and that the fire was accidental." The jury urged the colony to build smaller family residences and to provide some means of fire protection. It did not determine the exact cause of the fire, but the residents of Sointula had their own ideas.

At the far end of Melula's ground floor, there had been a large oven used to bake goods for the colony. Hot air pipes, some metal and some wood, ran from the oven down the halls, with smaller pipes branching off into individual rooms to provide heat. Several people thought that a blast of hot air had blown over a lamp and started the fire. Others felt that the heating system itself was the culprit, with hot pipes igniting dry wood. This had almost happened once before, and there was ample ventilation in Melula to fan a stray spark.

But even darker speculations were circulating. It was said that Bell had been sent by the government to examine the company books. There were rumours of embezzlement, and even accusations that Kurikka as president, and Oberg as treasurer, had burned the building deliberately to destroy the company ledger. Kurikka confided in a letter to Aili: "I have been transformed from a gentle deer into a big bad wolf. I suspect another but cannot prove anything."

Not all were against Kurikka though. Even Herman Hantula, who had lost his wife and four children, did not blame Kurikka for what had happened. "1 cannot add my voice to the disorder which now sweeps over Sointula. My beloved wife and children now rest with the others in a common grave. Into that tomb went all my joy. I do not blame anyone but all my hopes for a brotherhood of spirit are gone."

Speculation over the cause of the fire strained the commune, until the board called a special meeting to deal with the matter. The directors suggested that Kurikka and Oberg, at whom the majority of the slander was directed, take legal action against their accusers. Kurikka travelled to Nanaimo, but was informed by the company's lawyer that "those kinds of slanderous remarks belong to the order of the day. Anyone who works for the public should be prepared to accept such filth." This advice, plus the fact that legal proceedings would be costly and that the main slanderers had left the island, convinced Kurikka not to pursue the matter. He informed the board that although he would not be pressing charges, he did want the two men who had accused him of arson to be expelled from the Kalevan Kansa. Many members were reluctant to do this, and a lengthy debate took place. Determined to have his good name restored at least symbolically, Kurikka threatened to resign if the men were not officially expelled. In the interests of harmony the board agreed to his motion. Mäkelä, who had regained his eyesight, strongly opposed this decision, and the two men faced the first serious conflict in their friendship.

CHAPTER EIGHT

Sisu

Even though the clothes need mending
And the stew needs meat
The lengths of timber jump
When the donkey gives them a pull.
The sawmill operates
Vinetta whistles
As the machinery hums
And as the men strain.
This beautiful land
Will reward our troubles
But the freeloaders and the lazy
It will drive away.

Austin Mäkelä 1904

WITH ITS IMPOSING SIZE AND BASIC COMFORTS, Melula was both a physical and spiritual symbol for all that the colony stood for and hoped to achieve. Its loss, along with eleven lives, was a devastating blow that affected the colonists emotionally as well as economically. Damages from the fire were estimated at $10,000; if it hadn't been for the donations of food, clothing, cash and other supplies, the colony would have collapsed.

Finns, however, are noted for their *sisu*, a combination of self-reliance and fortitude, so in spite of their sorrows

The Kalevan Kansa Colonization Company executive committee, 1904. Standing: J. Felix Myntti, Herman Hantula, V. Vesa, J. Hintsa. Sitting: C. Ahonen, August Oherg, Abe Karmekangas, Austin Mäkelä, Matti Kurikka (at table), Andrew Järvinen, Jussi Padwo, Theodore Tanner and Francis Ilberg. In 1900 the Finns asked Kurikka to lead them to a better life; by October 1904 he had resigned as president of the Kalevan Kansa and left the commune under a cloud of recrimination and controversy. (SM)

and doubts the colonists began to rebuild. The large communal house was replaced with smaller, individual residences for families, and on Sundays and evenings a sleeping shelter was thrown together for the single men. Reviving their optimism and ambition, the Finns sawed rough hoards for a meeting hall, barn and warehouse, with a dining hall, kitchen, hospital, school, photography studio and inn scheduled for the near future.

For some the fire had ended their dreams of utopia. Discouraged by recent events, several members moved away, including Oswald Beckman. He took his family to San Francisco, where he established himself as an ear, nose and throat specialist, catering to the elite of Nob Hill.

In spite of the troubles and hardship experienced by those living on Malcolm Island, to the outside world Sointula was a philosophy as well as a place. Finns everywhere talked about the Kalevan Kansa, and near Fort Bragg, California, north of San Francisco, four families bought a section of land and named their commune Sointula, modeling it after the colony in British Columbia.

Three weeks after the fire the Kalevan Kansa held its annual general meeting, in a partially completed log sauna with ninety-three members present. Mäkelä emphasized the positive: "Though this year has been the most difficult in our history, much has been accomplished. Since the fire a score of dwellings have been built and we now have a pier so our mail and freight comes to us directly rather than through Alert Bay."

The annual report recorded 238 people living on the

On Saturday nights the Finnish colonists relaxed with plays, concerts, and debates at the Finnish Organization Hall, 1903. The band master sitting in the foreground is Voitt Peippo. (Dorse; SM)

The building that used to be Malm's sauna, 1992. Many Sointula babies were born in this building. In Finland saunas were considered an excellent place to deliver a baby. (Rick James)

island: 100 men (43 married), 50 women (43 married), and 88 children (53 boys, 35 girls). The first baby (Mikka Toiva Poutter, later known as Mike Poulton) had been born on October 26, 1902, and nine more babies were delivered over the winter. The financial situation, however, was still precarious. The treasurer's report showed income for the previous year as $20,794.78, with expenses of $20,762.40. The Kalevan Kansa had outstanding loans in the amount of $60,960.39, and nearly all of the capital equipment had been purchased on credit. Timber and land valued at $34,600.92 were the colony's biggest assets. A motion was passed to make the sawmill the colony's primary industry.

That spring, a barge with a tall, lathwork rack was

built to haul hay, and a mower and horse-pulled rake were bought on credit. Throughout the summer, the *Vinetta* hauled men, horses and equipment to tidal flats on the mainland, to cut wild grasses for livestock feed. On the island, close to seventy acres had been cleared, and where necessary drained by ditches up to three metres (ten feet) deep. Several of the colonists had their savings in a joint bank account, and there was talk of the Kalevan Kansa forming its own bank to lend money to others wishing to come to the island.

By fall a small shed had been built, and $1000 was scraped together to buy a more efficient printing press. The first Sointula issue of the *Aika* appeared on November 1, 1903, and by the end of the month the press was turning out 1500 copies every two weeks. Kurikka called the revised *Aika*, now in journal rather

A 1904 issue of the *Aika*, printed in Sointula. The *Aika* (Time) was Canada's first printed Finnish newspaper. The *Aika* was distributed worldwide and contained articles on socialism and theosophy. It also encouraged Finns to move to the utopian commune on Malcolm Island. (Rick James; SM)

than newspaper form, "a periodical of a broader kind." A typical issue contained articles by Kurikka and Mäkelä on topics ranging from theosophy, politics and temperance activities, to current events on Malcolm Island and in Finland. Often a humorous play such as Mäkelä's *A Night In Alert Bay* was included. The *Aika* provided a cultural base for the colony, and although anything could be discussed in the periodical, most of the articles attempted to create a feeling of unity and fellowship, and many encouraged other Finns to join the Kalevan Kansa and move to Sointula.

A new member had given the company $2000 to purchase a bigger donkey engine for the sawmill, leading both Halminen and Oberg to predict that the colony's financial problems would be over if they could obtain an operating loan for the next five years. On December 19, eighty members attended a special meeting where they voted to consolidate their debts by seeking a loan of up to $10,000, using colony buildings and equipment as collateral. The money would be used to purchase machinery and tools, especially the equipment necessary to construct a planing mill and to manufacture barrels for packing fish.

While the board of directors was trying to arrange a loan, a story about two wealthy Finns in Vancouver drifted up the coast. Rumour had it that they had discovered a rich copper field while hunting on the mainland. On his next trip to Vancouver, Mäkelä was instructed to find the men and convince them to join the Kalevan Kansa and to share their mining profits with the company. "There was a big sigh of relief when the men joined the Kalevan Kansa," Mäkelä said, "until I realized that they had not staked a claim or even collected any samples of the ore."

Mäkelä rented a boat and set out with one of the men to secure the claim. After a few days of sailing, they put ashore and started to walk inland. On the fourth day, Mäkelä found some gold coloured rocks, then he saw a thick seam of yellow

Sointula sawmill, 1904. The Finns built this mill by trial and error, but once it was in operation it could produce up to 10,000 board feet of lumber a day. (SM)

running through the river bank. He wondered if they had found not copper, but gold. They staked a claim and gathered as many samples as they could carry, but in Vancouver the assayer didn't waste much in the way of time or words. What they had, he said, "was a large quantity of sulfurated iron with no value whatsoever."

Since the colony wasn't going to be saved by the copper mine, and the board hadn't been able to get a loan, a couple of colonists agreed to use their savings to complete the sawmill if they would receive a share of the mill in return. All projects except logging were put on hold, and by early 1904 the mill was finished. Though the Finns could produce 10,000 board feet of lumber a day, marketing remained a problem. A mill owned by missionaries in Alert Bay supplied Cormorant Island's needs, and the *Vinetta* was too small to transport lumber to Vancouver. It was obvious that for the sawmill to be profitable, the Kalevan Kansa needed a larger boat. A short time later the *Aika* announced: "We are buying a new tug with an eight horse power engine. The *Lottie* will be paid for with $1,950.00 worth of lumber."

While the colonists were finalizing the purchase of the *Lottie*, the provincial government granted them full ownership of 640 acres surrounding the site of Sointula—if they would build a school valued at $2000 and have all classes taught in English. Although English, mechanics and other subjects had been taught on the island for some time, the Finns agreed to build the school by the following August.

The colony was still on slippery ground financially, but the company continued to extend itself with new projects, while Kurikka persisted in promoting his elaborate visions for social change. Not content to deal with the present and its problems, Kurikka proposed a plan for life, disability and unemployment insurance. In the *Aika* he wrote, "If every Kalevan Kansa member, no matter where they lived, could be insured for employment-related death and disability, that would make our company the most important organization in America." According to Kurikka's plan, members would be able to obtain loans for travel to and from jobs anywhere in the world. In the event of death or disability, widows, children or disabled workers could live in Sointula and be supported by the commune. "This is not a gamble," Kurikka said, "it is a responsibility to our family."

For some time he had also been talking about building a children's home, "a true school of life from beginning to end." As well as providing a superior environment and education for children, the home would free more women for the colony's labour force. As it was, women with young children were excused from the work which was normally required of every adult. Kurikka believed that women benefited from working rather than looking after children. "Giving birth is one thing and raising children another, often a mother is incapable or unfit to educate her own children."

The home opened in March 1904, with Lempi and Martti Myrtii looking after thirty children in a large three-room house. Parents had the choice of leaving their children at the home full time, or for day care only. If children were permanent residents of the home, the Kalevan Kansa purchased all their clothing and supplies; otherwise it remained the parents' responsibility.

At age seven, Arvo Tynjala was one of the older children in the home. "There were special beds that folded up against the wall during the day, then at night we put them down to sleep on. There was quite a bunch of us, we stayed there for days at a time. I tried to run away once but the teacher caught me."

The children's home freed ten women for work, but some, missing their children, complained about the standard of care. As usual, Kurikka addressed the problem in the *Aika*. "Women want to know how I can talk about raising children when I am not a mother, but is motherhood what teaches one how to raise children properly? Women carry their young, give birth, nurse them, and clean them, but doesn't a cat do the same for its kittens? To this day I have never heard anyone call a cat a good model for child rearing."

"Just because a women gives birth does not make her a competent mother or knowledgeable about what is best for the child," Kurikka continued. "If a chicken makes its nest in a dangerous place and you try to move the chicks to safety, the hen will squawk, peck, and do everything to prevent the move. That is exactly what these women who complain about the children's home school are doing."

While Kurikka's editorials on child rearing provoked heated debates, there was soon a new topic of concern. Ever since the Kalevan Kansa had been formed, membership applications had been processed at a steady rate. Halminen recalled: "I don't remember any memberships ever being refused, it was hard to tell much from an application anyway. Some people thought the Kalevan Kansa was a private business operated by Kurikka and there were many Finns in Vancouver looking for work. So our colony became a mix of people, some looking for jobs, others seeking utopia."

Originally there were two types of memberships. Those who paid their $200 fee in full and worked for the company a minimum of 150 days per year were called "inner members," while those who made a $50 down payment and pledged a full year's work were referred to as "outer members." In the early days of the colony, Kurikka suggested that members paying for their shares in labour should be limited, but there was no policy in place to deal with the matter. Although "foreign nationalities" were only allowed into the colony if they paid the full $200, all Finns who wanted to join the Kalevan Kansa were accepted, regardless of their financial situation.

In addition to membership fees, many Finns also donated livestock and farm equipment, and loaned or even gave the colony money. To date the Kalevan Kansa had borrowed $21,769.46 from its shareholders, and the board of directors worried that members leaving the colony would try to recover some of their money and assets. As this would destroy the already fragile economy, the board instructed Mäkelä to prepare an agreement which would clarify members' rights and the liability of the Kalevan Kansa. The agreement read: "By becoming an inner member I pledge to support the Kalevan Kansa's co-operative actions, joint ownership, and collective economic undertakings. I agree to not look upon my personal shares, contributions of work, money, or other donations from the perspective of those who live outside of Sointula, and understand that everything I contribute to the colony will be used for the purpose of founding and preserving our commune and its ideals."

The contract stipulated that since "this way of looking at things is foreign within British Columbia," any disagreements regarding personal property would be settled by the company rather than an outside court. By signing the agreement, members also agreed not to demand extra land or wages, and to work for the colony a minimum of 150 days per year.

These rules were to remain in effect until such time as the Kalevan Kansa was financially stable and could afford to pay yearly dividends. Some members of the colony disapproved of the contract and refused to sign. The majority, however, felt that it was their responsibility to make the company's internal affairs secure, and were willing to make personal sacrifices to do so.

Kurikka was in Vancouver in late spring when he saw a call for tenders to construct bridges over the Capilano and Seymour rivers. On the advice of Mr. Jacobson, a business acquaintance from Seattle, Kurikka placed a bid of $3000 with a non-refundable deposit of $150. The Kalevan Kansa was awarded the contract, but when Kurikka returned to Sointula with the news some of the colonists felt that his bid had been too low. Kurikka agreed, but insisted that since they would be using lumber from Malcolm Island the colony could still make a profit. "More important than making money," he added, "is the possibility of future contracts in the Vancouver area worth tens of thousands of dollars."

After a lot of discussion, and the preparation of a new estimate, many of the Finns felt that it would still be in the company's best interests to withdraw the bid, even if it meant losing the deposit. Kurikka, however, was adamant that construction proceed. To clinch the argument, he announced that the financial affairs of the colony were so desperate that all supplies, even food, would end if the contract was not taken.

CHAPTER NINE

Free Love & the Bridge Fiasco

I T WAS RAPIDLY BECOMING APPARENT THAT DESPITE the attractiveness of Kurikka's charismatic personality and innovative plans, his inability to transform his ideas into practical action eventually caused his followers to turn against him. Toivo Hiltunen, the *Aika* press operator in Sointula, had succumbed to Kurikka's heady charm when he heard him speak in Astoria, Oregon, in 1903. Hiltunen wasn't in Sointula long, however, before he became disenchanted both with life on the island and with the visionary who had led him there. To annoy Kurikka, the pressman littered the *Aika* with frequent and deliberate printing errors.

Misprinted or not, Kurikka's editorials never failed to provoke an emotional response. The motto of the *Aika* was "Freedom with Responsibility," and Kurikka personally advocated responsible freedom in the area of sexual relations. He chose a May 1904 issue of the journal to formally launch his campaign to alter the traditional roles of marriage. His interest in marriage and motherhood began many years earlier in Minna Canth's salon; now he was determined to free both men and women from their blind obedience to convention.

"Let us assist women into a position of freedom and responsibility," he wrote. "Let us build marriage on a foundation of ideal love and refuse to acknowledge a marriage which is not centered on love, goodness and tenderness." He urged "Kalevan Kansa men to declare only the rights of love not the chains of marriage" and told women that "they need not be ashamed of motherhood outside of marriage."

Kurikka believed that it was acceptable for men and women to live together without being married as long as they loved each other. Although he believed that sexual activity should not be limited to marriage, he did not approve of casual or promiscuous sex. "A man who lightly indulges in sex," he said, "should have a millstone tied around his neck and be drowned."

Far ahead of his time, Kurikka was not so much against the institution of marriage as he was opposed to the subservient role of women. He felt that women were treated as pieces of property by their husbands and that all too often marriage resembled a form of slavery rather than a partnership of equals. To those who disagreed with his philosophy he replied, "Marriage and morality are as different as the law and justice, and the church and truth. Just as capitalism appears to protect social organization, and the church to protect truth, so marriage appears to protect morality."

Kurikka's articles on the emancipation of women and sexual relationships outside of marriage generated a great deal of controversy both on and off the island. As was often the case, Kurikka's beliefs did not necessarily reflect the reality of Sointula. On the whole, the members of the colony were opposed to the idea of sexual freedom. They worried that rumours about free love would jeopardize their agreement with the government, which required them to "honour and obey the laws of the land."

Katri Riksman said, "Some believed that free love would produce superior children, though the majority argued that men would not be interested in supporting or raising these children. Although Kurikka had a lady friend on the island, there were no superior children to his credit."

Kurikka did have the support of the younger, unmarried men, and no one could ignore the fact that women were attracted to him. Women always made up a large part of the audience when he lectured, and comments about his animal magnetism and glowing good looks were common. Women's interest in Kurikka had been noted even in Australia, where a fellow Finn noted that "Kurikka was divorced, he liked women and women liked him. Their husbands however had other ideas and his frequent affairs caused constant friction."

Eventually Lundell, the Lutheran preacher from Extension, formally complained to the provincial government that, "Matti Kurikka is the leader of a socialist and atheist element and he personally advocates Free Love. All of his actions are moulding Sointula in that direction."

Concerned about the financial aspects of the government's agreement with the Finns, the Lieutenant Governor commissioned Vancouver lawyer Henry Sherwood to investigate Malcolm Island under the provisions of the Public Inquiries Act. Sherwood was instructed to determine if the Finns were making a bona fide effort to settle the island, or were just planning to harvest the timber and then leave.

Unaware that the government's concerns were economic rather than sexual, Kurikka attempted to prove that he wasn't promoting universal divorce by telling the Victoria *Daily Colonist*, "The state of marriage has existed before there was any church and it will continue to exist even when slave-like dogmas have disappeared from civilized nations."

He was more candid in the *Aika*. "Because of their dirty imaginations people believe that all sexual activity outside of marriage is criminal. They believe that sexual passion is animalistic and must be ignored."

Kurikka's biggest opponent over the role of women and sexual relations outside of marriage was his former best friend, Austin Mäkelä. The two men had never mended the rift that occurred after the fire, when Kurikka demanded that the Kalevan Kama expel his slanderers. Instead the chasm between Kurikka and Mäkelä deepened, and while they had disagreed before, now they argued constantly. Angry and frustrated over the foundering of his own marriage, Mäkelä complained that, "as a single man Kurikka is interested in all women and would like to see every marriage dissolve." He accused Kurikka of promoting a three-way marriage, where a woman would live with one man for intellectual companionship and another for physical activity.

The tension between Kurikka and Mäkelä filtered into the community, and soon everyone was arguing about free love and other topics as well. On the whole, life on the island was far more difficult than life in the outside world. Hard work was not yet rewarded with wages, and the food left much to be desired. Salt fish and potatoes were the mainstay of the diet, and for months at a time there was no sugar and only occasionally stewed prunes for dessert. Doing without luxuries was one thing, but doing without the bare necessities was another. Less dedicated members bickered among themselves, accusing one and then the other of eating too much or working too little. And even though Kurikka had assured the Kalevan Kansa that he had "hands as calloused as any," Matti Halminen noted that while everyone else performed heavy manual labour, "Kurikka did not seem to have any duties except for his talks."

Inevitably, some of the quarrels evolved into lawsuits between the company and its members. Lili Anderson—probably a widow who had become involved with one of the single men—felt that her reputation had been destroyed during the many arguments about free love, and requested compensation for damages to her good name, as well as the return of her membership fee. A committee elected to arbitrate the matter instructed the Kalevan Kansa to return the $450 that Anderson had invested in the colony. Herman Hantula, who had lost most of his family in the fire, asked for the return of his two horses and farm equipment. The committee refused his request, on the grounds that the company had spent more feeding the horses than they were worth.

The Kalevan Kansa was still in desperate need of skilled workers and most of all, in need of capital to make the colony viable. Not only was neither forthcoming, but Kurikka's mercurial nature and inability to face reality was becoming an increasing problem. On one occasion he begged the colonists to donate their rings, watches and earrings so he could convert them to cash; on another he returned from a trip to Vancouver with a portable lap organ instead of the expected food and supplies. The colonists' idealism was wearing thin, and while a certain amount of eccentricity had been overlooked and even expected before, now it was unacceptable.

A lot of energy and money was being expended with little in the way of rewards. Logging operations had increased but were still not creating much revenue. Attempts at stock breeding had been unsuccessful; a few cows had even died over the winter of 1903–04. The Finns had a fishing licence for Rivers Inlet but didn't have enough nets, and even though the government had given the Kalevan Kansa permission to build a cannery at Knight Inlet, there was no money to do so. More fields were being cleared, but so far potatoes were the only crop worth mentioning.

To raise some cash, Kurikka had a collection of his and other colonists' poems published in Vancouver. Titled *Kalevan Kansan Sointuja I* and *II* (Kalevan Kansa Songs of Harmony), the two slim volumes were filled with idealistic offerings such as *The Kalevan Kansa March, Malcolm Island Our Beautiful Homeland, Leave The Old Ways Behind*, and *Our Idealism Is Saved*. Kurikka took copies of the books with him on his speaking tours, where he devoted a portion of each lecture to reading the poems aloud and singing them to the tunes of traditional Finnish hymns. Altogether he sold 2500 copies. Although he swore that he made a full accounting to the company, there were rumours that most, if not all, of the money went into his own pocket.

Meanwhile, preparations for the construction of the

bridges in Vancouver had revealed major discrepancies in the original estimate. Both bridges featured 55-metre (180-foot) arches and the bridge over the Capilano River required a span of the same length supported on an 11-metre (36-foot) buttress. The bridges required exceptionally strong foundations, an item totally overlooked in Kurikka's bid. Another oversight was the fact that all building materials had to be transported over a kilometre from the dock, making it necessary to purchase a team of horses and a sleigh. Also, only a small sum had been allowed for miscellaneous items such as bolts and nails. This cost alone came to $1600. Even though the municipality of North Vancouver contributed $600 for additional supplies, the colony's total bill for extra work and materials came to $3000.

Everyone was involved in the construction of the bridges. Those who remained in Sointula sawed lumber and made do with even less as the colony struggled to transport the lumber and feed the men working in Vancouver. Families were separated for months at a time, and in an effort to meet the September 1904 deadline the Kalevan Kansa waived membership fees and advertised for additional workers in the *Aika*.

Instead of leading to "other contracts worth tens of thousands of dollars," as Kurikka had promised, the construction project required close to 9000 hours of uncompensated labour. One hundred men worked on the bridges for four months, receiving no wages and paying their expenses out of their own pockets. Worst of all, thousands of board feet of Malcolm Island's best timber went into the project. At one point Kurikka realized his mistake and encouraged the men to strike, but by this time he had lost his credibility and no one would listen to him.

Near the end of September the bridges were completed, and Kurikka and the others returned to Sointula. There was no respite for the weary workers though, for as soon as Kurikka set foot on the island the topic of free love was again brought up. This time Mäkelä openly accused Kurikka of having an affair with his wife, Elli, and blamed Kurikka for all his marital problems. Kurikka admitted that he was a close friend of Mäkelä's "civilized, honourable, and beautiful" wife but denied that they were having an affair. "Elli confided in me that she was going to ask Mäkelä for a divorce and that she wanted to marry another comrade whom she loved, but that man is not me." Arguments between the two men became vicious, and the board of directors suggested that they both leave the island for a while to cool off. Neither would go, so in an effort to resolve the situation once and for all, the board called a general meeting.

CHAPTER TEN

The Lesson of Sointula

HE FLAMES THAT HAD DEVOURED MELULA twenty months earlier had fuelled a growing undercurrent of dissension and distrust. In an isolated community, frustrations tend to be narrowly focused. As president and spokesperson for the Kalevan Kansa, Kurikka received a lot of attention and consequently most of the criticism. While the role of leader had initially been thrust upon him, now many had doubts about his abilities. Older colonists began to shift their allegiance to the more conventional and practical Mäkelä.

Concerns over the constitution, the status of private property and the question of free love widened the gap between the differing factions. Fully aware of the growing discontent, Kurikka worried that he might lose his position as president at the upcoming special meeting. Impulsive and proud, he chose to avoid that embarrassment by resigning on October 10, 1904. A few days later, Kurikka left Malcolm Island with approximately half the colonists. Those who believed in Kurikka went with him, while those who believed in Sointula remained behind. Each side felt wronged by the other and the air was heavy with angry words. As the boat and barge pulled away Mäkelä vowed, "I will dedicate the rest of my life to making you harmless to mankind!" Kurikka replied, "You curse me now but some day I will find a real Sointula."

In Vancouver Kurikka arranged rooms for his followers

in a hotel on Heatley Avenue, while he moved into a building that had once been the Kalevan Kansa's office. To his daughter he wrote: "Much has happened here. My separation from the Kalevan Kansa is the result of personal persecution but the best members follow me. The island with the buildings and machinery remain with Mäkelä and his supporters, and to them are also left the debts. I regret the split but feel that it was inevitable. Materialism in Sointula was becoming so brazen that it was impossible for a civilized person to stay."

Kurikka's departure, some say eviction, from Malcolm Island received mixed reactions from the socialist press. The Ontario *Väkäleuka* (Babbler) compared Kurikka's ego to Napoleon's and accused him of living off his ex-wife's inheritance. The reporter criticized Kurikka for his lack of consistency and "his one hundred faces . . . not one of them the same." Other newspapers, such as the *British Columbia Federationist*, defended Kurikka, "as a victim of infamous persecution, false blame, and vile lies." This article referred to the colonists who remained in Sointula as "hoodlums not up to the standards of socialist philosophy," and praised Kurikka as "a nobleminded man who gave his all for the welfare of Sointula."

Late in 1904 Kurikka obtained a shingle bolt contract near Webster's Corners, fifty kilometres east of Vancouver. His supporters placed a small down payment on some acreage in the area and formed *Sammon Takojat* (Forgers of the Place of the Sampo). Like Sointula, Sammon Takojat was to be a utopian, socialist society with an emphasis on theosophy and communal endeavors. But unlike Sointula, this commune was for men only.

Kurikka and twenty-four men moved to Sammon Takojat on January 1, 1905. They built a large one-room cabin from which Kurikka wrote Aili: "I have started a new commune and the members are all bachelors. Still I miss Sointula. Just think how it feels to leave machines and cultivated fields, the visible assets of four years' work, simply because your best friend has betrayed you!" Six weeks later, Kurikka departed on a lecture and fund-raising tour, but confided to his daughter that he had left certain problems behind also. "I have again had great difficulties to overcome. Enthusiastic materialists, my own followers, are agitating against me, but that has always been the reward of idealistic thinkers!" Kurikka was still on tour when he received a letter from the men at Sammon Takojat. They wrote that they were tired of being celibate as well as poor and informed Kurikka that women were now living at the commune. The letter ended by stating that his presence at Sammon Takojat was no longer required.

Not one to be idle for long, Kurikka went to Finland, where—even though Alexander I of Russia had granted the Finns freedom of language, parliament and religion—the PanSlavic Party continued to pressure Czar Nicholas II for Russification. The Finnish Social Democratic Party greeted Kurikka with enthusiasm and welcomed his talents as a writer and speaker. His popularity was short-lived, however, as he soon became known as a fiery instigator, unsuitable as a long-term leader.

At loose ends, Kurikka started the periodical *Elana* (Life), wrote *The School of Life II—The Idea of Sointula*, and began to indulge his interest in mysticism, astrology and seances. At the age of 43, having observed a marriage of conscience for some time, he married Hanna Raivo on May 23, 1906. Kurikka was proud of his new wife, who was fair, beautiful and twenty years his junior. In December Hanna gave birth to Kurikka's second daughter, Auli Annikki.

Two years later, having lost *Elana* due to financial difficulties, Kurikka and his family departed for the United States, where they settled in Penker, Connecticut. There Kurikka bought a small farm, raised chickens and wrote for Finnish American newspapers. Always in his thoughts were dreams for a new utopia. At one point he planned to purchase 300 acres near Vancouver and form a cooperative. When that failed,

Matti Kurikka in Penker, Connecticut, 1914. After he left Sointula, Kurikka developed an interest in seances, ouija boards and the occult. He was a prolific writer and continued to seek funding for a utopian settlement until his death in 1915. (Linnoila collection)

he tried to interest a friend in financing a women's commune. Kurikka still considered himself a director of the Kalevan Kansa, and as late as 1913 entertained plans for a New Sointula in Penker.

Kurikka and his family visited Finland toward the end of 1913, but he returned to Connecticut alone. Hanna complained that she was tired of living a life of poverty, while Kurikka accused her of being unfaithful. They argued over custody of Auli until she returned to Connecticut in 1914. Only a year later Kurikka collapsed while clearing some brush on his farm. A telegram to his family in Finland stated, "Kurikka died of heart failure."

Kurikka's efforts to form communes in Australia, Sointula and Webster's Corners, established him as one of the great utopian founders of his time. Few men have generated such tremendous energy and expectations, or pursued their dreams with such tenacity. But wherever he went, Kurikka's volatile personality always left a residue of resentment and anger. The image of the visionary as a scoundrel is one that still lingers today. Even in Sointula, the site of his largest commune, he is referred to as "a trouble maker," "an advocate of free love," or "the one who ran off with all the money."

Cool, deliberate, almost methodical, it was Mäkelä who stepped into Kurikka's role as spokesperson for the Kalevan Kansa. Mäkelä's steady demeanor inspired confidence after Kurikka's erratic and turbulent leadership. Those remaining on Malcolm Island readily dropped theosophy and embraced Mäkelä's more materialistic form of socialism. The colonists respected Mäkelä and perhaps more importantly, they knew what to expect from him. Unlike Kurikka, who advocated change via the heart, Mäkelä was a staunch Marxist who stressed the need to alter political and economic institutions. "Not a single struggle has been won by using spiritual weapons such as discussing, debating and voting," he declared.

He told the colonists, "The lesson of Sointula is that we live in a capitalist society. Proudly though we turned our backs on the capitalist world, we are still dependent on it in every way. The very first boat load of goods to reach the island was bought on credit and that has never changed." As for those who had left with Kurikka, Mäkelä referred to them as "the people who tried to make stumps lay eggs. Their *sisu* was admirable but *sisu* alone is not enough."

Faced with an enormous debt load and a greatly reduced labour pool, the thirty-six families struggled to earn a living with the sawmill. Even though the government's investigation of the Finns had noted that, "They are committed to the island and are just the people to make Malcolm Island one of the best settlements on the British Columbia coast,"

Mäkelä suggested at a December 5, 1904 meeting that the Kalevan Kansa rent eighty acre parcels of land to any members who were interested. That way, even if the Kalevan Kansa's agreement with the government collapsed, these properties would remain secure. By mid-December almost every family on the island had signed a lease. To curb expenses it was voted to stop publishing the *Aika*, and the printing press was sold for less than half of what it had cost. The last issue of the *Aika* was the end of a Finnish-language newspaper in Canada until the *Työkansa* (Work Folk) began publication in Ontario in 1907.

Kalevan Kansa workshops, circa 1910. The building on the left was the blacksmith shop, next to it was the machine shop. These two buildings were destroyed by fire in 1925. The small shed on the far right was later used as a sauna. The man standing on the left is Anton Tannini, on the right is August Täht. (Pink collection)

The Kalevan Kansa annual general meeting was held on February 5, 1905, with fifty shareholders present and an additional ten represented by letters of proxy. To encourage new settlers, the Finns decided to rent some of the eighty acre parcels for a dollar an acre and to waive the rental fee for the first twenty parcels. They also agreed that there would be no more inner memberships and that the company would compensate all work days with cash.

A couple of weeks later the board organized the sawing of what they called "hut lumber." Each member who took part in the project received 2000 board feet of lumber. The excess was planed and by mid-March 150,000 board feet were ready for market. The Kalevan Kansa still owned a building lot on the shore in North Vancouver and the directors instructed Andrew Järvinen, then manager of the Kalevan Kansa, to transport the lumber to the lot and sell it. With the proceeds, the company planned to make a $200 loan payment and buy food, clothing and shoes. Järvinen took the wood first to his property in Vancouver to unload his share of the lumber. Suspecting that the Kalevan Kansa was up to no good, the tow boat captain notified the colony's creditors who seized the lumber, and without bothering to verify the situation, sold the wood for a third of its value. Approximately $3,000 was lost as a result of Järvinen's carelessness.

In desperation, the board sent Mäkelä to Vancouver to make arrangements with the government to pay the Kalevan Kansa's debts. The colony offered the only unmortgaged asset it had, the return of the 640 acres that the government had granted to it. Within a few weeks, the Vancouver-based Dominion Trust company became the administrator of all property belonging to the Kalevan Kansa. The last general meeting of the company was held on May 27, 1905, with thirty-six shareholders present. Everyone agreed to stop work on all Kalevan Kansa projects and to divide the few remaining assets. Each resident received ten pounds of flour, one pound of pork, a few fish, a plate, a cup, and a saucer.

Dominion Trust quickly sold all the movable chattels of the Kalevan Kansa including the dairy herd, and formed the Marine Lumber company to run the sawmill. For a while, the Marine Lumber Company employed some of the Finns on a contract to provide lumber for canneries in Rivers Inlet, but even this fragile economic security came to an end when Dominion Trust closed the sawmill and moved it off the island. While a few of the colonists were paid to dismantle the sawmill, others vented their frustrations by vandalizing property that was no longer theirs. Late in 1907, the trust company sold Malcolm Island's forests for five dollars an acre and paid off the last of the Kalevan Kansa's debts. None of the Finns were paid for their shares in the Kalevan Kansa, and no one received any wages for the hours of labour they had done for the colony.

For all his ability and good intentions, Mäkelä lacked the charisma and imagination necessary to convince the out side world of Sointula's viability. Outgoing and well spoken, Kurikka had thrived on speaking and fund-raising tours, often returning with several thousand dollars. Reserved, and with a weaker grasp of spoken English, Mäkelä preferred the role of political commentator and writer rather than activist. Unwilling and unable to obtain further credit for the colony, he was content with a quiet life on Malcolm Island.

In 1907, Mäkelä took the position of lighthouse keeper at Pulteney Point, at the east end of the island. His leisure time was spent growing potatoes, raising dairy cattle, and writing under the pen name of Kaapro Jaaskelainen. Many of his short stories and plays are still considered hilarious today.

Even though the light station was eight kilometres from Sointula by boat, Mäkelä retained an active presence in Sointula. Vaino Honkala said that, "Mäkelä guided the commune until his death. He was our lawyer, our justice of the peace, and in social matters, our advisor. He attended community meetings and kept everyone on an even keel. He didn't let

people wander off the topic, or get too over-heated or enthusiastic."

Although Mäkelä is referred to as "the one who stayed
on Malcolm Island," at times he was editor of the socialist
newspaper *Raivaaja* (Pioneer) in Massachusetts, the *Toveri*
(comrade) in Oregon and the *Vapaus* (Freedom) in Ontario.
He even returned to Finland, where his political popularity
proved to be more alluring than Kurikka's. Although he was
elected to the executive of the Social Democratic Party, after
only a year Mäkelä returned to Malcolm Island (with his new
wife Esa) saying, "the only people in Helsinki are spies and
cordwood dealers."

After each stint in the outside world, Mäkelä eagerly
retreated to the seclusion of Sointula. He joined the Social
Democratic Party of Canada and later the Communist Party,
but even he admitted that, "I was not a very active partici-
pant." When asked to write an article on Canadian affairs for
a Finnish publication he replied: "You could hardly find a
less suitable person. I get some Canadian papers and although
I follow their affairs to some extent, I always feel that they
do not affect me at all." Even when Yrjö Sirola, a prominent
Finnish socialist and founder of the Finnish Communist Party,
visited Mäkelä in Sointula and attempted to stir him to action,
Mäkelä continued to limit his efforts to the written word.

Although both Kurikka and MakeHi were well educated and travelled, neither was suited to directing the economic affairs of a community struggling to establish itself in
the wilderness. Both men played important roles in Canadian
working-class and political history, and each made a lasting
impression on Finnish Canadians. Each possessed qualities
that the other lacked, but their philosophical differences and
the age-old problem of jealousy prevented them from working
together.

Looking back, Matti Halminen reminisced: "It is possible that we were all in some ways unsuited to build an idealistic

community but a large number of us worked towards it with faith and good will. We had come to Malcolm Island as if to school, to be cleansed and to grow spiritually. But this did not help us to organize our affairs. If we had possessed as much wisdom and practical experience as we had sacrifice and vigor, we might have done better."

CHAPTER ELEVEN

The Hard Part of Life

WITH THE LOSS OF KURIKKA'S DYNAMIC, IF ineffectual, leadership, and the end of the Kalevan Kansa's cooperative efforts, the colonists had to find a way to support themselves. "We older members of the Kalevan Kansa had sacrificed everything for the commune," Matti Halminen reflected. "When it collapsed we found ourselves on an isolated island on which there were few ways of earning a living."

The Finns still had hopes of farming the land. In addition to the communal potato field, each family had its own garden, a few chickens, and maybe a cow or two. Theodore Tanner, who had studied horticulture in Finland, planted a large garden and a variety of fruit trees. By patiently grafting awl pruning he eventually produced multi-fruited trees that bore apples, plums and cherries. He and his wife, Amanda, gathered kelp from the beach for fertilizer and put garter snakes in the strawberry patch to discourage bugs. Once a week Tanner rowed to Alert Bay to sell his produce, often joined by Matti Halminen carrying a couple of pails of milk and a pound or two of butter.

Even though the island's forests had been sold, there was another natural resource that could be converted into cash. Malcolm Island's mink were prolific and their coats were thick and glossy. The island became a maze of trap lines. "After we trapped the mink," recalled Tanner's youngest son, Teuvo, "we'd skin the hides and cure them, then ship the pelts

Picnic, 1914. (Malm collection)

to Vancouver where they were sold by the piece. It was quality fur but we never made more than pocket money from it."

The only industry to survive the death of the Kalevan Kansa was the blacksmith shop. John Honkala, a bell maker from Finland, forged iron from the early days of the colony until 1922. He was well known for his super-thin scythe blades, and filled the Finn's blacksmithing needs with a combination of creativity and practicality. But money was scarce, and more often than not Honkala was paid with a crock of salt fish or a sack of potatoes.

Farming, trapping and blacksmithing generated a few dollars, but the Finns desperately needed jobs that paid cash. "That's when the really hard part of life began," recalled Arvo Tynjala, "when the men had to look for work outside Sointula. Many had come directly from Finland and didn't know a word of English. The language problem was very serious." Groups of two or three men, if possible with someone who knew at least a few words of English, left the island in five-metre (sixteen-foot) row boats. They scoured each inlet and island between Vancouver Island and the mainland as far south as Seymour Narrows, looking for logging camps that were hiring. Arvo was a teenager when he joined the men in the boats. "Sometimes we'd circle around hundreds of miles without finding anything. We'd stay in empty loggers' shacks or we'd sleep on the beach. Some mornings there'd be six or seven inches of snow in the boat, but we just kept going."

The early 1900s were lean years and few jobs were available. Even though Sointula Finns were respected

Kaarlo Kaisla (white shirt) and friends deer hunting on Malcolm Island, 1916. The Kaisla family had a home at Pulteney Point. Kaarlo was artistic and often painted sets and scenery for plays at the hall. (Malm collection)

In 1912 the Tynjalas bought 86 acres on Kaleva Road and built this house. (Malm collection)

as hard workers, more interested in how much they could accomplish than how much money they could make, some of the logging companies were reluctant to hire them. Men from Vancouver were captive employees, at least until the supply boat turned up every week or so. But as Arvo pointed out, "We were kind of independent. We had our own boats, if something went wrong we could row away—we were noted for that."

Working in the woods was a rough job. The weather was usually nasty, many situations were dangerous, and living conditions were always primitive. Often as many as two dozen men slept in one large room heated by a barrel wood heater. Ropes criss-crossed the ceiling, and at the end of the day that was where everyone hung their wet and dirty flannel shirts, heavy pants and wool socks. According to Arvo: "It really stunk in there! We had to bring our own blankets, all the bunkhouse had was mattresses on hemlock springs. Nothing was provided by the logging company except the bedbugs, there was plenty of them! As soon as the lights went out you could feel the darn things moving around looking for you—it was fierce!"

Logging outfits operated mainly in the spring and fall, shutting down when the snow got too heavy in winter and the woods too dry in summer. While there was no other work to be found in the heart of winter, during the summer the sea was alive with salmon. Since 1902 the Finns had drag-seined for food fish on Vancouver Island at the mouths of the Clux-ewe and Nimpkish Rivers, which Arvo Tynjala remembered as "black clouds of fish" when the salmon were spawning. At that time, all fishing was done inside river boundaries, and there

August Täht and his wife at their home in Rough Bay, circa 1910, The Tähts were one of four Estonian families that bought property from the Kalevan Kansa. When the Tähts returned to Estonia (Mrs. Täht did not enjoy life on a remote island), August's cousin Alex Pink bought the property. (Pink collection)

was no limit on how many fish could be caught. The Alert Bay cannery floated a barge into the Nimpkish River and it was often filled with just one set—enough to keep the cannery busy all day. There were many summers when the Alert Bay cannery packed 14,000 48-pound cases of sockeye salmon from the Nimpkish River alone.

By 1906 the Finns were travelling north to Rivers Inlet, a major fishing area on the mainland, well known for its large runs of sockeye salmon. The 112-kilometre (seventy-mile) trip usually took three days, in double-ended rowboats equipped with two sets of oars. Once they reached the sheltered waters of the inlet, the Finns looked for a cannery that was willing to rent them a skiff for the six-week season.

Olavi John Anderson, better known as O.J. or Ole, was born in Sointula in 1913. He grew up hearing stories about the early days of fishing, and later became a fisherman himself. "It was all company-owned gear. Most of the time the skiff would be sunk, tied to the float. The fisherman would have to bail it out, then go get the floor boards and hatch covers from the net loft and fit them in place."

Treated with tar on the inside and painted cannery colours on the outside, the 8.5 to 10-metre (28 to 32-foot) skiffs sported either a cotton tent, waterproof until touched, or a hinged doghouse forward from the main bulkhead. Before primus stoves became popular a little "cod"—a miniature wood stove that burned bark—was the only concession to comfort. A week's worth of groceries and an anchor—sometimes just a rock and a piece of line—completed the outfit.

Opening day was usually the third Sunday in June. The fishermen rowed from the cannery float to the tow boat, which pulled up to forty skiffs at a time. When they reached the fishing area, skiffs were cut loose and the fishermen were on their own. According to regulations, fishing began at 6:00 p.m., but few of the men owned watches. The cannery fired a gun to announce the opening, but everybody usually just started fishing when they thought the time was right. In those days, fishing meant rowing a few strokes, then throwing a buoy attached to the net over the stern. The fisherman then rowed a bit farther, releasing more net as he went. Two or three sets were made each day, and the catch was stored in hatches at the sides of the boat. At dusk, a lantern replaced the company flag at the end of the net.

Arvo was fourteen when he went commercial fishing. "By the end of the day the floor of the skiff would be soaked. We'd splash some wood alcohol on the boards, light it and let it burn long enough to dry the water off." Once the floor was dry, the fisherman would erect his tent and fire up his little

Sointula school 1914–15. Teacher: John Stevens. Urho Tynjala is 4th from right in back row. Harold Malm (hat) is 11th from right in the back row. Hannes Myntti (frizzy hair below window) is the 3rd from the left in the front row. (Malm collection)

A string of skiffs being towed to the fishing grounds, 1930. As many as forty skiffs could e pulled behind one tow boat. When they reached the grounds each fisherman cut his skiff loose, hoping that the boats behind wouldn't run into them. (Salo collection)

stove. Dinner might be some warmed-up stew or a piece of fish fried with a potato. Matti Riksman always had a sack of dehydrated bread that his wife Katri had baked and dried on sunwarmed rocks. Katri's bread never got moldy, but Matti had to dunk it in coffee before he could chew it. Later, Sointula women shipped fresh bread to Rivers Inlet on the Union steamships.

At dawn, the fishermen pulled in their nets. How a net was picked up had a great deal to do with how easy it would be to put it back out. Ole recalled: "The nets were 50 mesh, 200 fathoms. They were heavy in those days because of the wooden corks and you had to haul the net into the skiff by hand. We used to split the net—drop the lead line at your feet and throw the cork line into another pile. The old-timers made a beautiful pile of it, every cork would sit just so."

Weekends the linen fishing nets had to be soaked in bluestone tanks for a couple of hours to remove the algae and

Hand-pulled gillnet boat, circa 1928. (Tanner collection)

prevent the net from rotting. But there was time for fun, as well. Canneries employed a lot of women, and almost every Saturday night there was a dance, often livened up by a jug of rum from a nearby bootlegger. Although Sointula was still temperance-minded, the Finns weren't above joining in the fun when they were away from home.

At the end of the season, the canneries tallied up the number of fish delivered by each boat. For many years sockeye, large or small, were sold for seven cents each. "They didn't weigh the fish in those days, they just counted them and kept track that way," Ole said. "One year two ladies of ill repute travelled to Rivers in a gillnetter. They charged first ten, then twenty sockeye for their services. When the fish were tallied at the end of the season those ladies had the high boat for the inlet."

Although fishing was physically demanding and filled with

risks, the Finns thrived on it. Here at last was an occupation where their capacity for hard work was more important than money or training. In the 1920s, small horse-powered Easthope and Vivian gas engines began to

Laurie Jarvis and wife Helmi, later known as Granny Jarvis, circa 1925. (Hufnagel collection)

replace sails and oars, increasing the number of boats as well as their mobility. Where there had been 700 boats fishing the inlet in the past, now there were up to 2000.

Toward the end of the decade, ownership of skiffs began to shift from the canneries to the fishermen. For many, it was cheaper to build a boat than buy one. One by one, huge cedar-planked sheds appeared on Malcolm Island's beaches. Their massive doors swung wide to the sea, reaching into it with ribbons of steel track. Although Sointula soon gained a reputation as a boat-building centre, in reality many of the shops only built one boat, then concentrated on maintenance and repairs.

John Anderson, a fisherman, boat builder and writer, moved to Sointula in 1911 and bought the original colony cabin. He established the first of Malcolm Island's nine boat yards in 1918, and by 1951 Anderson Marine Ways had built over 600 vessels, ranging from simple row boats to the sixteen-metre (52-foot) seiner *Twin Sisters*. "At one point we were building eight skiffs a week, all 28 feet long with cedar planking and fir bottoms," recalled Ole Anderson, who worked at his dad's boat shop between fishing seasons.

While gas engines made fishing easier, the nets, wet and often heavy with salmon, were still set and hauled by hand. It was a backbreaking job that strained the muscles and resulted in stiff, arthritic hands. It often took veteran gillnetters several hours just to straighten out their fingers after a day of fishing. As well as being hard on the body, hand-pulled nets also meant that boats could only fish in slack tide, or not at all if the weather was bad.

Laurie Jarvis, then Jarvelainen, moved to Sointula when he was nine years old. As a teenager he worked as a logger, and spent his days surrounded by logs, chokers and cable spools. Later he opened a boat yard, and was recognized as an inventive repairman as well as a boat builder. During the summer months Jarvis joined the gillnet fleet, where he did his share of complaining about the cumbersome hand-operated nets. Then one day he noticed an abandoned spool cable on the beach and thought, "Why not haul nets in the same way loggers reel in cable?" By 1931 he had designed and built the first gillnet drum out of yellow cedar.

Charlie Peterson, a logger and fisherman who married Theodore Tanner's daughter Sally, was in Rivers Inlet when Jarvis made his first set with the drum. "The net tangled so badly that they had to take the drum off with a derrick at Wadham's Cannery," Peterson said. "No matter how carefully Jarvis reeled in the net, it snarled again and again. It took the derrick and four men to undo the mess before he discovered the trouble."

On hand-set nets, the lead line was shorter than the cork line. For the net to roll onto the drum without tangling, all Jarvis had to do was lengthen the lead line. His friends Helen and Lauri Wilman helped him calculate the proper size of the drum and core for the volume of the net, but drive gears were still a problem.

Sointula fisherman Burt Peterson watched his dad and Jarvis experiment with the gears. "They tried a dry friction but that burned out too fast. Then they installed bevel gears from the rear end of a Model T Ford, but there was too much load for a smooth operation. Next they tried the gears of a truck but they were too hard to back up. Finally a rear end system off a Model A Ford solved the problem."

Jarvis worked for over a year to perfect his drum, then placed a patent on his invention and converted his boatyard into a drum manufacturing plant. Now that they could rapidly set and haul in their nets, fishermen were no longer limited by the tides and weather. Orders for drums poured in, and Jarvis was hard-pressed to meet the demand. It wasn't long before other gillnetters, impatient or reluctant to pay the $25 fee, began building their own drums. Jarvis hired a lawyer and went to court. He won his case, but all he could do was force

Cleaning fishing nets in a bluestone tank, 1929. Fishing nets had to he cleaned every week to prevent rotting. They were soaked in the bluestone solution for a couple of hours, then rinsed well so the caustic chemicals wouldn't dissolve the nails in the boat. (Salo collection)

Fish boat with tent shelter, 1930. When a fisherman was on the grounds his skiff was work site, kitchen and bedroom. The tents leaked and the skiff floor was wet more often than it was dry. (Salo collection)

people to remove the drums from their boats. The legal fees mounted, and after a few years Jarvis dissolved his patent. Even though it revolutionized the fishing industry world-wide, the drum was nothing more than a large thread spool, a concept too simple to make the patent effective. Toward the end of the 1930s another Sointula fishermen, Ted Davidson, took Jarvis' idea one step farther and adapted and installed a drum on his seine boat, the *Who Cares*.

The "hard part of life" was over. No one had much in the way of money, but logging and fishing provided modest incomes for most, and Sointula's economy was more stable than it had ever been under the guidance of the idealistic Kurikka. Going away to work did nothing to weaken the Finns' commitment to Malcolm Island. Instead, it reinforced their strong sense of community. They were proud of the fact that they were Sointula Finns and felt that this distinguished them, not only from the outside world, but from other Finns as well. This unity gradually solidified, and the void left by the Kalevan Kansa was filled by an interest in British Columbia's emerging left-wing political parties.

CHAPTER TWELVE

Apostles of Socialism

E VEN THOUGH THE KALEVAN KANSA HAD FAILED, the Finns had not lost their desire to create a new social order. Now that the colony was financially stable, they began to look for practical ways to express their ideals. Hoping that socialism would provide the sense of purpose and identity that the Kalevan Kansa had promised, they began to contact like-minded groups. And still confident that Sointula could be a model for other communities, they became involved in Canadian politics.

The Sointula Socialist Club was formed in 1907 to support the Socialist Party of Canada (SPC), whose constitutional goal was "to transform capitalist property into the collective property of the working class." Mäkelä and John Rivers, a Finn logger who lived in Sointula for a while, joined forces to organize a Sointula SPC local. Rivers informed the SPC that, "we are all socialists in theory but as long as we stick with theory we cannot expect to accomplish anything. We are forming a local but do not expect to make many converts as everyone here is already a socialist except for one or two thick heads."

In May 1908, Rivers attended the SPC inter-provincial convention in Fernie, where he attempted to have a Sointula party member run as a candidate in the upcoming federal election. A lack of funds prevented this, and an SPC secretary noted that "one of the year's heaviest expenses was the printing of the constitution in Finnish—but the desirability of Finns as party members more than made up for the cost." The language problem was enormous, and in an effort to eliminate the massive amounts of translating, the Finns organized themselves as a separate arm of the party.

The SPC praised the Sointula local for holding regular meetings for men, women and children. The December 4, 1909, edition of their newspaper, the Western Clarion, declared, "If only our Anglo-Saxon members had half the zeal of the Sointula Finns!" Politics was serious business in Sointula. Everyone was expected to support the SPC; financially and otherwise. When three men happened to mention that they had cast their ballot for a capitalist candidate, they were promptly expelled from the local.

Although they were respected for their discipline and whole-hearted enthusiasm, the Finns from Sointula and other

Sointula's main street complete with free range cows, circa 1913. The cow lying ill the middle of the street is Salos' cow, Rachel. At the far left is the old red school house, which was moved and converted into a chicken coop when the new school was built in 1928. (Malm collection)

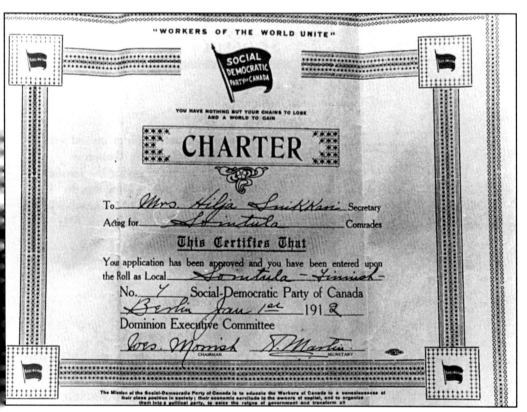

Sointula's Charter for the Social Democratic Party of Canada 1912. After their experiences in the Dunsmuir coal mines, Finn immigrants were quick to band together with others against the capitalist system. (Rick James; SM)

locals were called "clannish foreigners" when they began lobbying for changes in party policy. The Finns argued that the SPC needed to take an active role in improving conditions for workers, while main line party members felt that the SPC should concentrate on educating the masses. Conflict between the predominantly British leaders of the SPC and the Finns escalated, until by 1911 the entire Finnish membership had either been expelled from the party or withdrawn in protest.

That same year, Finns from Sointula and elsewhere joined the newly-formed Finnish Socialist Organization of Canada (FSOC), which later became the Finnish section of the Social Democratic Party of Canada (SDPC). As well as spreading the word via "apostles of socialism" (one of whom

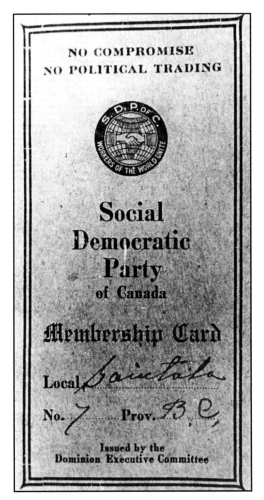

NO COMPROMISE
NO POLITICAL TRADING

Social
Democratic
Party
of Canada

Membership Card

Local *Sointula*

No. 7 Prov. B.C.

Issued by the
Dominion Executive Committee

Sointula Finns united with their fellow Canadian workers under the banner of the Social Democratic Party. An SDP membership card. (Rick James; SM)

was Matti Kurikka), the FSOC attempted to unite isolated communities of Finns and to enrich their lives with cultural activities and education.

With the outbreak of World War One, immigrant organizations that expressed socialist and anti-war sentiments were viewed with suspicion. In 1918 as part of the Red Scare, the Canadian government banned or censored all foreign-language publications and declared both the SDP and the FSOC illegal organizations. A year later, the FSOC was allowed to reorganize as the Finnish Organization of Canada (FOC), as long as members agreed not to associate with the SDP. Throughout Canada, Finnish settlements deeded their community assets, usually their hall, to the FOC for cultural and educational purposes. The Sointula local of the FOC used its hall for plays and concerts, and held classes to increase the knowledge and skills of its members.

The FOC eventually became affiliated with the Worker's Party of Canada (WPC), later renamed the Communist Party of Canada (CPC). Almost everyone in Sointula was a member of the FOC, and since the FOC required its members to carry a CPC card, almost everyone in Sointula was also a member of the Communist Party. The Vancouver *Province* called Malcolm Island "the home of the Finnish Communistic Colony."

Alfred Williams, grandson of the Riksmans and Honkalas, said: "In the old days the FOC was for the working class. There were meetings every Sunday night and kids age ten and older were expected to attend. Someone would read the news from the FO in Toronto and we would discuss what needed to

Mrs. Savola's funeral cortege in front of Finnish Organization Hall, circa 1913. First man at left front is Alex Anderson, next to him stands Peter Hilton. The man at the right of the coffin is Mr. Savola. (Malm collection)

Above:
Otto and Jenny Luck and Otto's mother. Otto was the first president of the Sointula Credit Union. (Malm collection)

Left:
Jenny Luck and Edla Malm. Edla Malm was Sointula's midwife, and is credited with delivering over 200 babies. (Malm collection)

be done around the community."

According to Ole Anderson the FOC "was definitely connected with the labour movement. If there was a miners' strike back east, the FO would let us know and we would take a collection or put on a show and send the proceeds to the strikers. When BC loggers went on strike we collected sacks of potatoes and vegetables to donate to their families."

The Finns were not strangers to the concept of collective action. After the Kalevan Kansa folded, many found jobs at the short-lived Suquash coal mine located nearby on Vancouver Island. The Finns decided to strike for more money, but the miners from Vancouver refused to join them. When the Finns went to picket the mine, the manager wouldn't let them on the site. Wiljami Honkala said, "We told the boss, 'you can't keep us from below the high water mark,' and went down to the beach. We lined up with all our brass instruments and blew our horns so hard that even the tree tops waved!"

Now the Finns had the FOC and the growing union movement to support them in their struggles for higher wages and better conditions. Arvo Tynjala recalled early attempts to unionize workers. "They were trying to organize a loggers' union but it took awhile. There was the Lumber Workers Industrial Union (LWIU), it was promising but it didn't get spread around to the camps enough to form a real force. Then there was the One Big Union (OBU). There was quite a lot of talk and the feeling that something was being done. We knew these groups existed but it didn't effect us much. Later I was a delegate for the LWIU for a year or two but the headquarters moved to Ontario and it kind of died away."

The LWIU, formed in 1919, was the forerunner of the International Woodworkers of America (IWA). One of its founders was a Norwegian named Arne Johnson. A large man with a stern look about him, Johnson was secretary for the LWIU before he resigned to become president of the IWA Loggers Local 1–71. He spent most of his time visiting remote

Francis Millerd Fishing Company Cannery at Sointula, 1926. (BCARS 68782)

camps, frequently hiring fishing boats from Sointula to take union organizers up and down the coast.

It wasn't unusual for camp bosses to deny union representatives access to the camps. When that happened, Johnson would get the loggers' attention with the fog horn and speak to them from the boat. Often he sneaked into a camp and more than once he was threatened by camp managers. One of these altercations resulted in Johnson being charged with assault.

At far right is Millerd Cannery dock, circa 1930. Francis Millerd operated a cannery in Sointula in the late 1920s. For a time after the cannery closed, the building was used as a sawmill. (Pink collection)

The prosecution argued that Johnson had entered the camp and "terrorized" the men, while the defense attorney said that loggers who paid room and board had the right to receive visitors. The court found Johnson not guilty, but fined him five dollars for technical assault. After this incident the union initiated the Arne Johnson Fund, which was used to promote the union's right to approach workers. In the early 1940s Johnson, one of many union organizers blackballed by major logging companies, moved to Sointula, where it was easy to find work with small-scale logging operations.

Logging was not the only industry where changes were taking place. Commercial fishing had become the Finns' primary means of earning a living and the Rivers Inlet sockeye provided a semi-reliable income, depending on the size of the salmon run and the price the canneries were willing to pay. In his memoirs Matti Halminen noted: "Still the fishermen are dependent on capitalism and give their catch to the canners. To start cooperative action we have formed a union."

An article in the February 1917 issue of the *British Columbia*

Bruno Kaario. Kaario was an avid wrestler, who had to have a steel plate put in his head after an accident as a dockyard worker. (Malm collection)

Federationist reported a mass meeting held in Sointula to organize Rivers Inlet fishermen. "The organization aims to protect fishermen against exploitation by cannery owners, to secure better prices for their catch, to protest against restrictions which now inconvenience fishermen, and to provide better working conditions." The Finns named their independent union the United Fishermen of BC (UFBC) and called for a strike. "The cost of everything was going up but the canneries were only offering fifteen cents a piece for fish," Arvo Tynjala said. "We went on strike for twenty-five cents and eventually settled for twenty-two."

Despite the Finns' efforts, the UFBC folded in 1924. There were other unions they could have joined, but preferring to organize and control their own activities, they decided to form a fishing co-op. In December 1928, they formally applied to register the British Columbia Fishermen's Cooperative Association (BCFCA). Although other fishing co-ops had operated for a season or two, the BCFCA was the province's first registered fishing co-operative. A constitution was written, in Finnish, and fishermen bought $25 shares. One of the first things the BCFCA did was purchase a bulk order of salmon gillnets. These nets, which were supposed to provide a huge savings for co-op members, turned out to be virtually useless. The knots slipped frequently, changing the size and shape of the mesh, and worst of all, the nets were made from short fibers. These hairy tendrils caught and reflected any phosphorescence in the water, instantly revealing the nets' presence to the fish. Some fishermen attempted to burn these short hairs off, but after several nets went up in flames they were all thrown away.

The gillnet fiasco resulted in the co-op facing a loss of $3000 in its first year. The Finns still had faith in their organization, however, and were convinced that strength would come with numbers. They encouraged fishermen outside Sointula to join, and when most of the members were from the Lower

Mainland, the head office moved to Vancouver. President Bruno Kaario and secretary-treasurer Otto Ottava were the only Sointula Finns to remain on the board of directors.

To obtain a canning licence the co-op bought Francis Millerd's cannery operation, complete with Millerd as manager. It was only a matter of weeks before there was trouble. Some complained that the Finn directors were "hamstringing Millerd and ruining the co-op," while others accused Millerd of refusing to cooperate. Part of the problem was that—as a former private businessman—Millerd was not used to answering to anyone other than himself. He thought the co-op's process of meetings and general consensus was too slow and cumbersome.

Finns in Sointula, 1930. Left to right: John Frederickson, Theodore Tanner, John Malm, Uuno Salmi, Gus Savola, John Tynjala, Willie Ahola. (Tanner collection)

Aeroplane view of Sointula, 1927. (Pacific Airways Ltd.; Belveal collection)

The board found themselves divided between those who were not fluent in the English language and those who didn't really understand cooperative principles.

The tension climaxed at the end of the 1930 fishing season, when twenty Sointula fishermen went to Vancouver for their annual shopping trip. Known for being soft-hearted and generous, Ottava issued the men cheques, hoping that funds would be available to cover the drafts before they cleared. The Finns cashed their cheques immediately and the BCFCA bank account was overdrawn. Already suspicious of the Sointula faction, fishermen in Vancouver spread rumours that the co-op only paid men from Malcolm Island, while Sointula fishermen believed that only those who travelled to Vancouver got compensated. A general meeting was called and the entire board was replaced, although several members defended Kaario, saying, "he is a remarkable man, completely unselfish and true to his beliefs." The new board tried to keep the co-op alive, but the Depression left little money for anyone to buy shares and the BCFCA folded in 1932.

The hopeful years of the 1920s came to an abrupt end with the Depression. The canneries slashed their prices, and as one Sointula fisherman put it, "Fishing is more or less a struggle between hope and despair." A two-week strike in 1932 saw prices rise for a year or two. Then, in 1936, they were reduced to 40 cents a sockeye. With most fishermen losing money rather than making it, those who fished British Columbia's central coast agreed to strike.

Lester Peterson, a fisherman raised on the northern end of Vancouver Island, recalled: "The 1936 strike was a good example of Finnish influence. Never before had there been such a united show of fishermen. We just sat and watched the fish go by. It was as if there was a storm blowing there were so many fish jumping in Schooner Pass. The leaders who held us together during the Great Strike were Sointula fishermen."

"To show solidarity during the strike of 1936 all the Sointula gillnetters tied their boats together," Teuvo Tanner recalled. "The boats stretched from Pulteney Point on Malcolm Island clear across to Vancouver Island. It was just about impossible to keep the line straight or steer, but we kept it up all the way from the lighthouse to Sointula."

Many fishermen sacrificed the entire season that summer but the following year, for the first time, the fishing industry agreed to pay for fish by the pound. The fishermen had a choice, either seven cents a pound or forty cents a fish. To commemorate the event Sointula women embroidered a tapestry that contained the names of over eighty members of the Fishermen and Cannery Workers Industrial Union of Canada, the majority of whom were Finns, who participated in the strike of 1936.

Re-piling nets on a table seiner after they've been mended, circa 1938. (Salo collection)

While the Finns in Sointula and other parts of Canada made significant contributions to both the labour and socialist movements during the first part of the century, the 1930s were a difficult time. Work was scarce, wages were poor and the rapid formation and then collapse of unions and co-ops led to an unsettled feeling. Faced with mass layoffs in the logging industry and reduced prices for fish, many Finns became frustrated with their battle to overcome Canada's capitalist system.

Sointula Finns were particularly vocal in their political endeavours, leading the media to refer to Malcolm Island as the "Canadian hotbed of communism." Austin Mäkelä was particularly well known. After his death from a hemorrhage in February 1932, the Ontario Vapaus hailed him as "one of the most faithful members of the Communist Party of Canada." In

Sointula, after gathering at the FO Hall, a long line of mourners walked the coffin the kilometre to the cemetery at Koti Point. At the front of the procession flew a standard hearing the hammer and sickle.

Two years after Mäkelä's death, the Vancouver *Province* stated that, "for 30 years the Finns have maintained a communist state on Malcolm Island. Today they probably know less about what's happening in Canada than the Soviet Union. They seldom leave the island but keep in touch with Russia, their spiritual home." At that time Finnish newspapers in North America were covering the progress of the five-year

The Young Pioneers of Canada escort Austin Mäkelä's body from the Finnish Organization Hall to the cemetery, 1932. Leading the procession and carrying the flag with the hammer and sickle is Albert Maki. A few years later Maki disappeared in Soviet Karelia. (Pink collection)

socialist plan of Soviet Karelia on the border of Finland and Russia. With the full support of the FOC, Stalin urged all communist Finns to "help him build a strong socialist Karelia." Like an epidemic, Karelia fever spread through Finnish communities, often prompting entire families to emigrate. Still longing for a socialist utopia, Finns from Sointula were seduced by Stalin's call. Once in Karelia, however, they found a shortage of food, shoddy living quarters and, echoing their reception in Canada, hostility and antagonism from local residents. Many Canadian Finns were victims of the violence, imprisonment and murder that took place during the 1935 purges. Tauno Salo said: "Erie Pouttu and Albert Maki went to Soviet Karelia from Sointula. They were just young men. They weren't gone very long when they disappeared and nothing was ever heard from them again."

The majority who emigrated to the new utopia felt that it was the mistake of a lifetime, and found that it was much easier to enter Soviet Karelia than to leave it. "It wasn't easy to get out," Salo said, "but some made it. They took all your money when you got there and then you couldn't leave. John Anderson and his family went, but they hid their money in their youngest son's shoes. That's how they had enough money to get out."

While some struggled in Soviet Karelia, many Finnish Canadians simply retreated into their communities rather than face a suspicious and sometimes hostile outside world. Remote and insular, Malcolm Island was an ideal refuge.

CHAPTER THIRTEEN

No Churches . . . No Troubles

BY THE 1940S, HOMES STRETCHED ALONG Malcolm Island's southern shore from Pulteney Point to the bluffs at the end of Kaleva Road, with a few houses in Mitchell Bay as well. The population had swelled to over 450, mostly direct descendants of the original settlers. A blend of relatives and neighbours, the community was close-knit and protective. Marriages, births and funerals were considered community events; invitations were neither issued nor needed. Family ties were strong and children were given responsibilities at an early age. "Chores were very important," Tauno Salo recalled. "They had to he done. When I was old enough I helped at haying time and I delivered milk every day before and after school. We didn't have milk bottles so we used three or five pound lard cans."

Although families lived and worked as individual households, colonists were united by their political beliefs, language and culture. Communal dinners remained a part of island life long after the Kalevan Kansa. Late Sunday afternoon everyone gathered at the Finnish Organization Hall. The building was finished with rough planks and the tables and benches were more of the same, but the well-scrubbed oilcloth, the smell of *kalalaatikko* (salt fish and potatoes) and the buzz of conversation made the room feel friendly and comfortable. Richard Michelson remembered going to these weekly dinners as a youngster. "The schoolteacher ate at the hall on Sundays

Sointula halibut fleet, 1940. (Salo collection)

too, but she got to use good dishes and even got butter. Us kids would try to sit as close to her as possible so we could watch her eat that butter. It came in big square boxes and most of the time the darn stuff smelled bad."

Rather than being discouraged by their isolation, the Finns welcomed the challenges of life in a remote area. Survival meant becoming adept at whatever needed to be done, and it was not unusual for a man to be a fisherman, logger, farmer, carpenter and musician, or for a woman to gather hay, milk cows and also to be a cook, seamstress and writer. For most, employment continued to follow the seasonal patterns of fishing and logging.

Hard and tireless workers, the Finns devoted the same degree of energy and enthusiasm to their leisure activities. The transition between work week and weekend began late Saturday afternoon in the sauna. To the Finns the sauna is a way of life, a ritual that refreshes the spirit as well as cleanses the body. A simple structure, a sauna usually has a change area and a room heated by wood in an enclosed firebox that is covered with stones. People sit or lie on tiered benches soaking in the heat, occasionally throwing water on the stones to make steam. After perspiring, the skin is sometimes slapped with leafy branches to stimulate the flow of blood. A typical sauna ends with the body being cooled down with a dip in the ocean, a roll in the snow or a bucket of cold water.

Traditionally a communal affair, the sauna is best when enjoyed in the company of family, friends and visitors. News is exchanged, tired muscles relax, and perspective is gained on any problems that may have accumulated during the week. A

Sointula fishermen Gordie Mannix and Harold Malm on a table seiner, possibly the *Tarzann 1*, October 1940. (Salo collection)

Picnic at Rough Bay, circa 1932. Drinking tea: Mrs. Savoia, Mrs. Wilman. Sitting at table: Amanda Wartianen, rear: Mummu Parkoo, Irene Michelson. Girl with glasses: Selma Salmi. In front of table left to right: Sid Wilson, Adelaida Pink and Isabelle Salmi holding Dickie Michelson. (Pink collection)

person is expected to emerge morally clean as well as physically. Those not familiar with saunas, however, often considered the practice indecent. An August 1938 article in the Vancouver *Province*, titled "A Coastal Eden," noted that, "Malcolm Island settlers still preserve their custom of having both sexes bathe together in the raw. It is not unusual to have the sensibilities disgusted on a coastal cruise by witnessing this bathing in the altogether."

In Finland hell is a cold place, and heat is sacred. As well as cleaning the body, the warmth of the sauna is supposed to dear the mind of evil thoughts and free the body from disease. While some claim that Sointula saunas have cured tuberculosis, arthritis and paralysis, everyone knew that the sauna was the best place to have a baby. According to the Kalevala, even Jesus was born in a sauna.

After Dr. Beckman left the island, Edla Maim attended most births in the role of midwife. Edla and her husband John had followed Kurikka, first to Australia and then to Sointula in 1902. Edla delivered Tauno Salo in August 1912. "I was born in Maim's old birthing house, it is still standing today. Mrs. Maim was the midwife here for many years. She delivered over 200 babies and only lost two."

Originally Sointula had a community sauna located on the beach below the FO Hall. The building was divided into two sections, one for women and children and one for men. When not being used for bathing, the sauna served as a communal laundry. Having a sauna was considered one of life's necessities—just as

John and Edla Malm digging potatoes, 1945. Potatoes were the first crop the Finns planted, and salt fish and potatoes is still eaten in Sointula. (Malm collection)

The Sointula band, 1932. Top left to right: Toivo Tynjala, Peter Hilton, Henry Honkala, Alex Anderson. Center left to right: Toivo (Tom) Ahola, Urho Tynjala, Wester Siider, Arvo Tynjala. Bottom row left to right: Harold Malm, Otto Luck, Arthur Snikker, Wiljami Honkala (later known as William Williams), Uuno Salmi. People travelled from miles away to hear the band play. (Tanner collection)

important as owning a house or boat—and eventually most families built their own.

Next to the sauna, the most significant community building was the FO Hall. Nearly every night of the week kerosene lanterns spilled light from the windows of the big building on the hill. "We didn't have any money to go anywhere or any car to run around the streets with—there were no streets. We had to make our own fun," Ole Anderson declared.

Most Saturday nights a play was performed in Finnish, complete with lavish costumes and scenery all sewn and constructed by volunteers. The Finnish Organization of Canada had a catalogue of over 300 full-length plays written by popular Finnish and Finn-Canadian writers, and it rented scripts for a nominal fee. These dramas focused on politics and the labour movement, but many of the plays performed in Sointula were written by residents. One of the most popular, *On Board Ship*, was written by Ole's father, John. This musical comedy poked fun at sailors and their reputation for having a girl in every port.

"My dad was one of those fellows that was never still," Ole recalled. "If he wasn't working in the boat shop he was reading or writing. Often people would ask him to write a song or poem for an upcoming performance. I remember lots of

Alex Anderson's house, which started out near the school and was later moved to Rough Bay. Because often it was easier to move a house than build a new one, houses were pulled onto log rafts and floated to another part of the island. (Belveal collection)

times in the shop he'd get a verse in his head and write it on a piece of plywood or on the back of a piece of sandpaper. Come 5:00 we'd be hunting all over for those things."

Most of the plays had three acts and ran for several hours. Two or three times a year, on New Year's Eve or other special occasions, a five-act production was staged. A cast of fifty was not unheard of, and the play often lasted from 8:00 p.m. to midnight. A committee assigned roles, and if someone was unable to play their part it was up to them to find a replacement. Vaino Honkala said, "We used to go to the hall four or five nights a week to practice. We had a lot of good

Sointula Drill Team with exercising sticks in front of Finnish Organization Hall, 1934. Physical fitness and exercise was an important part of life in Sointula. Many people attended exercise classes throughout the week and on Sundays at the FO Hall or Athletic Club. (Pink collection)

singers so our plays usually had lots of songs. During the performance the hall was packed and there would even be people standing in the aisles. It attracted a lot of people from outside, they didn't understand the words but they understood the action. They begged us to translate some of the shows into English."

After the play there was a break for coffee in the downstairs kitchen. The women took turns baking, and fifteen cents bought an endless supply of strong coffee, *pulla* (cardamom spiced sweet biscuit) and sandwiches. Then the dancing began. The original band formed in 1917 and continued in one form or another throughout the 1940s. There was almost always an accordion, a piano, a set of drums and a combination of saxophones, trombones and trumpets. If a travelling salesman was in town and happened to have an instrument, he was invited to play too.

Alfred Williams played the accordion. "We played ballroom, old time and modern jazz. Everybody wanted to dance so you had to have a beat. We'd get maybe $2 a night for playing, but we didn't play for the money, we played for the good time."

The whole community attended the show and dance. A couple of mattresses were laid on the floor of the women's cloak room for sleepy children to rest while their parents danced until 4:00 or 5:00 a.m., stopping every couple of hours to fuel up with more coffee. Word of Sointula's Saturday night dances reached Vancouver Island and the mainland, and people from other settlements often showed up for the fun. Couples and families were welcome but, unless they were known, single men were treated with suspicion. At every dance two or three Finns were designated as "police" and a room in the hall was reserved as a "jail." Theft was never a problem—all the women left their purses on a table by the door and nothing was ever reported missing—but if an outsider paid too much attention to a local woman there was a fight. If strangers left the dance or were wandering around town, it wasn't unusual for a couple of men to follow them just to make sure they didn't cause any trouble.

Sundays were devoted to more serious pursuits. Though missionaries appeared on the island from time to time, the Finns remained firmly opposed to any organized church or religion. Instead they spent their day of rest developing their minds and bodies. Lessons in Finnish, English and Esperanto, a universal language created from several European languages, were taught, as well as classes in bookkeeping and first aid. An athletic hall was built in the mid-1930s, and the library was installed upstairs, while the main floor was used as a gym. Every Sunday morning Theodore Tanner walked from his farm in Rough Bay to coach children in the art of debating and various types of exercises. A travelling gym instructor once commented that the "Finns were the most enthusiastic gymnasts he had ever seen."

The quick and nimble Tauno Salo spent a lot of time in the athletic hall. "There was some equipment but not much. We used to make group pyramids. The oldest and strongest men would get in a circle and hold onto each other. Then the others would climb up until everybody was standing on somebody else's shoulders. We went four men high, almost to the ceiling. I was often the top man, it was quite a trick to climb to the top without upsetting the balance."

In the afternoon, depending on the time of year, groups met to go ice skating on Maim's pond, hike to Pulteney Point or row to Vancouver Island for a picnic on the banks of the Cluxewe River. If the weather was miserable everyone met at the FO Hall to listen to readings and debates. "Someone would put up a question, political or otherwise and we'd argue the pros and cons of it," Ole said. "We were supposed to discuss the question until we all agreed on an answer—everyone got involved and there were lots of heated discussions. If we weren't debating we were talking about the cooperative movement."

Tauno Salo goose hunting, 1930. It wasn't unusual for Tauno to put in a full day at the co-op, dance all night at the FO Hall, then go hunting at dawn. (Salo collection)

Back in 1909 the Finns had decided to form a co-op, to protect Sointula from total dependence on the capitalist system. By that fall, they had translated the Co-operatives Act, elected a board of directors and formed the Sointula Co-operative Association. A store was built with volunteer labour and shares were sold for $100, with most families making a $20 down payment. Theodore Tanner was elected president and went to Vancouver to purchase the store's first supplies of flour, salt and sugar. More stock was acquired when the co-op bought out the small store that Peter Hilton had been running from his living room. The Sointula Co-op opened on December 4, 1909, with twenty-six members. Though the ledger showed a net loss of $50 at the end of the month, the monthly report (written in Finnish) stated, "We look to the future with hope."

For the first time since the Kalevan Kansa, the Finns

The original Sointula Co-Op store opened on December 4, 1909. Built with volunteer labour, the store provided groceries, hardware and a place to exchange news. In many ways it took the place of the Kalevan Kansa and became the unofficial governing body of the island. (Salo collection)

had a central organization to which virtually everyone belonged. As Urho Tynjala, Arvo's younger brother, said: "The co-op did everything here. It took the place of local government and for years it basically ran the community." As well as providing groceries, livestock feed, dry goods and hardware at five percent above landed cost, the store also contributed a portion of its yearly profits to the library, cemetery and other community projects. When a new library was needed (aging pioneers found the steps to the upper level of the athletic hall too steep), it was built on property donated by the co-op.

Salo started working at the co-op in 1936. "The freight came on the Union steamship, you could ship up to 100 pounds from Vancouver to Sointula for 55 cents. The ship unloaded at a big building at the end of the dock, then the freight was hand-trucked to the store with a four steel wheel heavy truck Later we used the co-op delivery truck, a Chevy Light Delivery 1929 model, and were able to deliver 40 or 50 sacks of grain at a time. Everything was in the same building, groceries, chicken feed, lumber, gas and oil."

Meralda Pink was a co-op employee for thirty years. "In the old days we had a really big crew. The store was a happy place, we all spoke Finn and were good friends. Once we had a bookkeeper from Scotland and a butcher from Ireland and we couldn't understand either one of them!"

Alex Pink and his daughter Meralda and Willie Ahola haying with the assistance of the gentle Tommi, circa 1934. Meralda hated raking hay, as it meant that she couldn't go swimming with the other children. (Pink collection)

Frank Lehtinen and Tauno Salo taking freight from the dock to the Sointula Co-op with a four wheel cart, April 1936. People regularly travelled from northern Vancouver Island and adjacent coastal areas to shop at the Sointula Co-op. (Salo collection)

When a fur buyer from Prince Rupert discovered that Sointula had a surplus of dairy products, he convinced the co-op to begin shipping milk and eggs up and down the coast. Most families had at least one cow and everyone raised chickens. Some families had as many as 400 hens, prompting a visitor to estimate that "Malcolm Island is home to over 10,000 chickens." It wasn't long before ten to fifty cases of eggs were leaving the island each week. Vaino believed that, "It was the marketing that really built up the co-op. They started shipping cases of eggs, 30 dozen in each case. Different people made butter too and sold it by the pound. In the spring if they had a lot of chicks they would keep the hens and ship the roosters live to Rupert."

The Sointula Co-op reached its peak just before World War Two. Alfred Williams said, "People came from all over to shop at the co-op. It had a fine hardware store and fishermen from as far away as Port Hardy would come here to rig up their boats." *The Fisherman Magazine* called the Sointula Coop "the biggest and most up to date department store on the coast between Powell River and Prince Rupert."

A fire destroyed the original store in 1933, and a new one was built in six weeks. A construction crew was paid fifty cents a day, with dinner and afternoon coffee added for good measure. When that building became too small in 1953, the current two-and-a-half-story frame building was constructed. The new co-op had a bench outside, soon a favourite spot for old-timers to sit and talk politics (after too many arguments the bench was removed) and a room upstairs for visiting doctors and dentists.

Harry Blake and Tauno Salo in front of the Sointula Co-op storage shed with the delivery truck, April 1936. (Salo collection)

Unless someone was seriously ill, for many years health care on the island was of a self-sufficient nature. Dr. Beckman left in 1903 and Edla Maim limited her services to delivering babies. If someone needed a doctor they either went to Alert Bay or Vancouver, or waited for a travelling doctor to show up. "If you had to go to the hospital in Alert Bay you went by fish boat or water taxi," said Laurie Jarvis' daughter, Diane Hufnagel. "The stretchers didn't fit in the cabins, so the head was put inside and people would stand outside and hold a tarp over the feet." In the early 1950s Harold Pickup, the physician in Alert Bay, began going to Sointula every two weeks. Pickup was one of those old-fashioned country doctors who was willing to do everything from pulling teeth to looking at the family pet. His office/examining room was on the second floor of the co-op,

When the original Sointula Co-op was destroyed by fire in 1933, the Finns constructed this building in six weeks. The work crew was paid fifty cents a day plus dinner and afternoon coffee. (Salo collection)

Athletic drill team giving a demonstration, 1938. Leading the group is instructor John Fredrickson. (Tanner collection)

Sointula women's drill team performing in Alert Bay, 1938. (Tanner collection)

but if a person was too sick or too old to climb the stairs, Pickup saw them on the main floor, often using the vault for a bit of privacy.

The new co-op building also housed the credit union. When the Sointula Credit Union opened in 1940, everyone deposited some money to show their support. One year later most of the money was still sitting in the accounts, and the credit union had only loaned out a little over $300. The inspector of credit unions shook his head over a membership that made deposits but didn't bother to make withdrawals, let alone borrow any money.

For many years the co-op annual and semi-annual meetings were major community events. Known as "eating meetings," sessions opened with morning coffee and often continued well past midnight. The store and school closed and women spent days preparing food. Most of the adults attended the meetings, spending hours discussing what was happening around the island and making plans for the future. "Everyone voiced their opinion and people weren't afraid to get up and say what they thought," Alfred noted. "They did that instead of talking behind somebody's back afterwards." Hannes Myntti, manager of the co-op from 1939 to 1962, said, "The co-op was a centre of vigor in the community and the annual meetings were bigger than Christmas."

The other important social occasion in Sointula was May Day. Traditionally a celebration of spring, by the late nineteenth century May Day had become a time to honour workers with parades and political demonstrations. May Day was a special time in Sointula when Meralda Pink was young. "That was the only holiday that we really celebrated and we waited for it all year. That was the day we all got new clothes. If there was only one time a year that you got new clothes, May Day was it."

The day began with a parade down First Street. Later, school children would sing and read poems and stories aloud at the FO Hall. Each year, Ole Anderson's mother helped him memorize poems for May Day. "There was a competition for kids age six to twelve. You had to know your poems by heart. If you won, you might get as much as $2, that was big money then." In the afternoon everyone moved to the athletic field where children and adults competed in disk throwing, shotput, broad jump and other games. Tauno Salo frequently won the children's skipping contests and decathlon. "It was exciting to watch the adult games," he remembered. "In one contest two men stood on a log that was about four feet in the air and swatted at each other with gunny sacks filled with wet hay. It was hard to keep their balance and those bags were heavy. Sooner or later one of the men would fall off the log and the other man was the winner."

"There was an old cedar tree at the field with a little platform part way up," Meralda recalled. "All the old boys would get up there and give speeches. It was almost like those fellows on soapboxes in London's Hyde Park. They'd get excited and angry and holler back and forth. May Day was also the day we got ice cream. Once a year they brought it in by Union steamship, all packed in big tubs surrounded by ice. It was a real treat."

May Day anchored the Finns to their socialist roots.

They looked forward to it as a time to celebrate everything they had accomplished. For many, the 1940s was Sointula's golden age. People had jobs, enough money to get by on, and life was pleasant and satisfying. As Sally Peterson said, "Sointula was a safe place to raise children. We depended on ourselves and had values. There was no serious trouble, people left their doors unlocked and their tools on the beach."

Ole added, "There was no church, no policeman, no beer parlours, and no trouble in those days."

The Sointula band in front of the speaker's platform, May Day, 1938.
Left to right: —, —, Alfred Williams, Alan Hilton, Vic Adams, Donald
Haapala, Eric Mäkelä, Edsel Kaario, Gordon Campbell, —. May Day
was the major holiday in Sointula for many years. The celebration ran
from morning to night, beginning with a parade and athletic competitions
and ending with a play and dance at the hall. (Salo collection)

Everybody Knew Everybody

FOR OVER FIFTY YEARS, SOINTULA'S MAIN LINK with the outside world was the Union steamship. Once, sometimes twice a week, freight, mail and passengers were picked up or unloaded at the community dock. The schedule varied, depending on the weather and what happened at other stops. Aileen Wooldridge remembered waiting for the steamship as a small child. "It seemed like whenever my family went to Vancouver the boat would come in the middle of the night. We lived out of town so we'd go to someone's house near the dock and just sit in their dark living room waiting for the steamship to come in."

No matter what time the boat arrived, it was the signal for activity. At the sound of the ship's horn the postmaster, Felix Myntti, would roll out of bed and walk down the hill with his wheelbarrow and lantern to collect the mail. "Even though it was late almost everyone met the boat," Felix's granddaughter Loretta Rihtamo recalled. "You could go on board and buy a newspaper or something to drink. They were a treat to travel on too—they had white tablecloths, silverware and gongs to announce the meals. It cost $13 for a first class stateroom and three meals. The only disappointment was the pancakes. They were big and fat, not thin like the Finnish ones I was used to."

Travelling to "town" was an extraordinary event; except to go fishing or logging most people remained close to home. One woman, busy raising a family, never left the island

The Union steamship *Cardena* docking at Sointula, circa 1948. The building in the foreground was used for many years as the library. The Canadian Imperial Bank of Commerce used to send a representative from Port McNeill once a week to set up banking facilities amid the books. (Belveal collection)

in seventeen years. While trips of any distance were made by Union steamship or fish boat, the Finns still relied on their double-ended rowboats to visit friends and shop at the co-op store. As John Anderson noted, "The sea is our highway, we have boats but no roads."

The rowboats were sturdy but open to the elements; the wind and tides dictated times to travel, and during winter's southeasterly storms it was often impossible to get from one part of the island to another. Using "picks, shovels, and oldtime community spirit," islanders built half a mile of road themselves, but as Anderson observed, "Every winter the roads became more suitable for rice paddies than for traffic."

In many areas, particularly Rough Bay and Kaleva, what was called a road was really nothing more than a cow path with some of the muddier sections covered with rough planks.

"That's what you walked on or you fell in the mud," Meralda Pink reminisced. "We usually got our groceries by rowboat but once when I was five years old I had to walk to the store by myself. There were cows and thistles everywhere. The cows didn't chase you but the bulls were something else!"

Charlie Peterson brought the first vehicle to the island in 1922, a 3.5 ton Federal truck with hard rubber tires. Charlie delivered Meralda's piano from the Union steamship, and for many years the Federal was used as the island freight truck. By the early 1940s, there were enough cars on the island

Sointula, June 1941. John Anderson's boat shop work crew gathered in front of his house. Standing left to right: Eino Pakala, Hannes Myntti, Tony Anderson, Donald Haapala, Hannes Kulmala, Oiva Halminen, Ted Tanner, Willie Oksanen, Lennie McKay, Olavi Anderson,. Sitting: Reino Tanner, John Anderson, Uuno Salmi, Ted Anderson. Child in the back is Donnie Anderson. (Tanner collection)

Janet and Ted Tanner with their Model T, 1939. (Tanner collection)

to justify some government funding for road improvements. Better roads meant ten kilometres of gravel surface, running along the south shore and connecting with a network of logging roads. In the past everyone had walked or rowed to the store, stopping to talk to everyone they met; now they drove and waved, or parked their vehicles in the narrow street to chat.

Eventually some sections of the road were covered with asphalt. "Once we had pavement they had to keep the cows off the roads, their hooves were too hard on the pavement," Meraida said. "We had a fellow who was like a dog catcher only he caught livestock instead." Paved roads also meant that people could drive faster, and in 1951 the Welfare Committee requested that the speed limit be posted at fifteen miles per hour.

Around the time that the footpaths were being widened to accommodate vehicles, English was beginning to replace the familiar sounds of Finnish. The provincial government had provided Sointula with a schoolteacher in 1904, with the understanding that classes would be conducted in English, but when Aileen Wooldridge started school in Sointula in 1940 she was the only child in her class who could speak the language fluently. "My grandparents spoke English because they had lived in the States and Saskatchewan," she said. "In school I did a lot of interpreting for the teacher but once we were outside we all spoke Finn." Finally one teacher banned the speaking of Finnish on the school grounds, which forced the children to become bilingual. The school, working off-island, and a small influx of outsiders increased the use of English, but it wasn't until World War Two was well under way that it was heard on a regular basis.

British Columbia's early Finn immigrants avoided participating in World War One, but by the 1940s most of their children had been born, or at least raised, on Canadian soil. Members of the new generation felt patriotic toward their homeland, and many volunteered for the armed forces. In Sointula the Finnish Organization Hall was decorated with Victory Loan posters and photographs of the King, Queen and Winston Churchill, while a recording of "God Save the Queen" was

Pioneer Logging Company, 1937. The Pioneer Logging Company truck-logged on Malcolm Island from 1934 until 1937, when they moved their operation to Port McNeill. (Salo collection)

Ethel Hukkala hunting from a dugout canoe, 1937. Ethel and her parents lived at Pulteney Point. (Tanner collection)

played before and after events. Speaking English became the popular thing to do, and some people anglicized their names. The three Honkala brothers, Vaino, Henry and Wiljami, became known as Wayne and Henry Homer and William Williams.

The post-war years brought a new sense of prosperity to the island. Alfred Williams recalled: "The war changed everything. When I came back from the Air Force everything seemed different. All of a sudden everybody had money."

A unionized fishing fleet was earning more than it ever had before, and larger disposable incomes brought modern consumer goods and services. "It seemed like things started to change with hydro," Aileen Wooldridge said. "When the BC Power Commission brought electricity to the island in 1951, it was seen as one of those improvements that would make life easier."

Clean, quiet and convenient, electricity replaced the coal oil and gas lamps, as well as the noisy generators that some had used to produce their own power. BC Power Commission strung their lines as far as Meralda Pink's Home in Rough Bay. "I remember the first night we had electricity.

Everyone had just a few little lamps but every light in the whole town was lit!"

Five years later, the North-West Telephone Company began installing telephones. Headlines in the January 25, 1956, Alert Bay Pioneer Journal hailed Sointula's telephone system as the first bilingual exchange in British Columbia. Fluent in both Finnish and English, Phyllis Michelson and Lillian Erickson handled all calls through a switchboard located in a duplex near the co-op store. Service was available from 8:00 a.m. to 10:00 p.m. daily and 4:00 p.m. to 8:00 p.m. on Sundays and holidays.

Out of the hundred phones installed, eighty-two were

Phyllis Michelson was one of the first switchboard operators when Malcolm Island received telephone service in 1956. Those working on the switchboard were fluent in Finnish and English. (Alert Bay *Pioneer Journal*, January 1956; SM)

party lines with up to seven residences on each line. Bonnie Nelson was seven years old when her family got a telephone. "We had a crank phone on the wall. Our number was 23R, R meant a party line. It was a big deal when we got dial phones that you could use 24 hours a day."

With telephones, people no longer had to leave their homes to talk to others. When television arrived, they socialized even less. Visiting back and forth had always been the primary form of recreation on the island, and although movies replaced the weekly dances, plays and athletic demonstrations at the FO Hall in the mid-1930s, at least everyone had still gotten together in one place.

"TV really changed the lifestyle here," Bonnie admitted. "We got one when I was a teenager. The reception was terrible—the screen was just snow. You couldn't see or hear anything but everybody was glued to the television trying to watch Peyton Place."

Loretta Rihtamo agreed: "Television changed everything. We don't have movies up at the hall anymore and everyone seems to have lost the gift of the gab. People don't take part in community activities the way they used to either, now they just stay home and sit in front of the TV."

And even when people did get together, the flavour of community events was changing. Although Sointula was founded on the principles of temperance, some alcohol had always been consumed. There was no liquor store on the island, but a bottle of vodka could be ordered from Vancouver by mail. Bootleggers were scattered all along the coast—a few fermented their own alcohol from salal and huckleberries—but on the whole, Sointula's temperance ideals were strong and the drinking of spirits was frowned upon. Those who did imbibe usually did so at home or discreetly stepped outside the hall for a nip during a dance.

Tauno Salo said: "Drinking wasn't a problem in the old days, although a few did it. It is hard to believe that people

Lennie Pohto barbecuing salmon at Sointula Salmon Days Festival, 1978.
In the late 1960s, Sointula's major celebration moved from May Day to
August, when the salmon fleet was in nearby waters. (Rick James)

can change so much in such a short time. Mäkelä was a very
good man but when he started drinking he was one of those
who couldn't handle liquor and would make a fool of himself
in public. He didn't approve of drinking either really."

As part of the post-war prosperity, the public consumption of alcohol was soon accepted at dances and other
community gatherings. The laws were strict regarding alcohol
and minors, so a dance would be held in the FO Hall and the
bar would be next door at the athletic hall. Later the bar was
moved into the kitchen in the lower level of the FO Hall.

Bonnie talked of "big open weddings at the hall that
everybody, all the kids, the whole family would attend. Kids
could even go to New Year's Eve dances, as long as the liquor
was served downstairs in the kitchen. Then they wanted to

Sointula Salmon Day Parade passing in front of Sointula Co-op, 1978.
(Rick James)

have liquor upstairs too, so kids weren't allowed at dances
anymore."

In the late 1960s Sointula's major holiday, May Day,
was shifted to August. Where the original community celebration had emphasized plays, speeches and games for children
and adults, the new Salmon Days featured an afternoon beer
garden and a cabaret-style dance. Diane Hufnagel stated that
"In the old days there was not one drunk up at the hall, unless
maybe an outsider came in. Now people won't go to a dance if
there isn't any booze."

As well as temperance, Matti Kurikka and the Kalevan
Kansa had also advocated "freedom from priests, churches,
and all the evils of the outside world." One reason the Finns
emigrated to North America was to escape the heavy taxation
of the Lutheran Church, which was not above confiscating the

only asset of value, the family cow. While a few people on Malcolm Island had religious leanings, most boasted that they "did not want or need a church." The general consensus was that "each person worship or not as they please." When someone died, Hannes Myntti or Urho Tynjala would say a few words at the cemetery before the body was laid to rest.

A couple of times a year, a missionary might spend a day or two on the island. A June 1941 article in the *Pioneer Journal* reported that, "The chaplain on the MS *Columbia* conducted a service in the Sointula Hall which was attended by 40 people," but it wasn't until 1948, when Alf and Margaret Bayne sprang a leak in their boat, that religious gatherings began to take place on a regular basis. The Baynes were part of the Pacific Coast Children's Mission headquartered on Quadra Island, and spent their time travelling up and down the coast teaching non-denominational Bible studies and

Katri Riksman celebrating her seventieth birthday, 1949. Riksman was the second Finnish woman on Malcolm Island. She arrived in 1902 and made Sointula her home until shortly before her death in 1969. She wrote for many magazines and newspapers under the pen name *Isoäiti* (Grandmother). Her last article was published when she was 89 years old. (Williams collection)

Christian songs. While the *Go Forth* was being repaired at Anderson Marine Ways, the Baynes became friends with Mamie Peterson, Emily Hilton and Laila Butcher. Mamie, a staunch Lutheran, and Emily, a Baptist, had moved to Sointula in the early 1940s; Laila had been born and raised on Malcolm Island. Despite their different backgrounds, the three women were united in their desire for some sort of formal religion, and asked the Baynes to hold Bible classes in the school. The Baynes obliged, and Sointula became a frequent stop for them on their trips up and down the coast.

In October 1952, when a Vancouver Lutheran minister went to Sointula to conduct a funeral for a woman who had recently immigrated from Finland, the *Pioneer Journal* headlined the obituary, "Prayers for Church at Sointula." An indignant John Anderson responded: "That article may express the opinions of the newcomers who arrived here a year or so ago from Finland but it does not correspond with the feelings of our pioneers who landed here 50 years ago. The statement that 'the people of Sointula have long prayed for a church' requires correcting. We have never prayed for a Church. We could have built one long ago if we had wanted to but we have managed quite well without one."

Disagreements over the need for a church continued, with some people meeting on a weekly basis to do "the Lord's work" and others complaining about "the religious newcomers." In the latter part of the 1950s, Pacific Coast Children's Mission lay pastor Lloyd Wiebe moved to the island to provide pastoral leadership, and by April 1, 1961, the Sointula Community Church had been built for the "benefit of those who wish to participate in church or Sointula Sunday school work." The congregation was described as Independent Inter-Denominational Evangelical Christians.

People involved with the church admitted that, "there was some opposition and a bit of a fuss all right when the church was built, but if our Creator wanted a church, worldly

Sointula pioneers, 1958. Left to right standing: Willie Ahola, John Malm, Felix Myntti, Alex Pink, John Mantta, Marcus Jamkkola. Sitting: Amanda Tanner, Mrs. Lanqvist, Katri Riksman, Amanda Pakkala, Amanda Wartianen, Gustava Hilton. (Tanner collection)

people couldn't stop that." A resident from the anti-church faction said: "It was mostly newcomers who started the church but there were some who had been born here too. The original settlers wanted to get away from organized religion and most of us supported that. There was a lot of grumbling when the church was built. A lot of people said 'Well we've got a church, I guess the next thing will be the police.'"

In a village where people do not lock their doors at night, petty theft is a sign of changing times. "We didn't have any police here in the old days," Wayne Homer pointed out. "The community was the caretaker of law and order. When somebody did something stupid there was no need of legal court, a public meeting was called to discuss the issue. There

Sointula breakwater and Millerd fish camp, 1976. (Rick James)

was no jury, just Mäkelä and someone else. They listened to both sides of the story and then voted to see which statement they wished to accept."

"And that was it, even for murder cases," Wayne continued. "I remember one case—the murderer was a mother. She had a baby out of wedlock and she didn't want it to live so she drowned it. Women were the judges in that court, no men were needed. They listened to her story and decided that she was not responsible for the act, that she was overwrought and nervous and didn't know what she was doing. She didn't even have to leave her grown son's house. She was allowed to live with him for the rest of her life."

Aside from this case and a murder/suicide where two men were killed in a drunken argument over a woman, most trouble on the island was just youthful mischief and pranks. Once Tauno Salo and Dave Davidson rode two of Tynjala's boars down the main street amid much squealing and shouting. Large, placid milk cows were frequently switched for small, cantankerous beasts, and one Halloween some boys managed to get a cow down the school stairs and lock it in a booth in the girls' washroom. But now people were worried about reckless and drinking drivers, and complained that tools left on the beach sometimes went missing.

"Around 1965 the RCMP from Alert Bay began visiting Sointula on weekends," Bonnie recalled. "Someone would see their boat coming and spread the word. This gave the teenagers a chance to get ready for fun and games. The cops rented the postmistress's car to get around in and pretty soon some teenagers would roar through town and get the cops to chase them out onto the logging roads. They played hide and seek out there for hours. I don't think the cops caught many of them."

By the late 1960s, there was little doubt that the character of Malcolm Island was changing, but the residents were still close. Looking back, one resident reflected:

"Sointula was the kind of place where everyone felt like family. If anyone needed help, it was given without a person having to ask. Everyone knew each other's business, just like any family, and helped when necessary and offered advice whether it was wanted or not."

As Ole Anderson put it: "You knew everyone in the community. When you saw a man coming down the street, you knew where he was coming from, you knew where he was going, and you knew what he was thinking about. Everybody knew everybody."

CHAPTER FIFTEEN

Back to the Land

MEETING THE BOAT FROM OUTSIDE WAS always an important part of Sointula life. In 1958 the Union Steamships were replaced by the *Island Princess*, a vehicle ferry that travelled between Sointula and Kelsey Bay once a day, hoisting cars on and off its deck with a large crane. When the *Island Princess* began unloading strange looking people in the late 1960s "meeting the ferry" took on a whole new meaning.

Jenny and Jim Green were operating an art gallery in San Francisco's Haight Ashbury during the era of "free love" and "flower power" when Jim was drafted. The Greens piled their possessions into a Volkswagen van and made their way north seeking refuge and a safe place to raise their infant daughter. "We got off the ferry in Sointula in the middle of the night and there were lights and people everywhere," Jenny recalled. "It was 1968 and it seemed like half the town had stayed up all night waiting for the boat to come in."

"After we had been in Sointula for a few weeks we went to our first function at the FO hall," Jenny continued. "We opened the door and all this wonderful music came pouring out. At the top of the staircase were a couple of drunks brawling, they fell down the stairs and landed at our feet. It felt like we had stepped back in time into the wild west."

Sointula residents gawked at the newcomers' funny cars, baggy clothes and heads, and frowned at the long, dirty

An old homestead with sauna and boat shed, 1974. Many saunas were located on the beach so only a few steps were required for that refreshing dip in the ocean. (Rick James)

hair that was prevalent on the men as well as the women. While non-Finns had moved to the island before, they had never arrived in such large numbers and they had never looked so unusual. The Greens and others like them were full-blown hippies, and most of the people in Sointula had never even seen hell-bottoms before. As well as looking odd, the new people acted differently too. They perplexed co-op clerks by asking for "health food," and it didn't take the Greens long to determine that they were the only vegetarians in the entire fishing village.

The majority of the new people congregated in the outlying areas of Mitchell Bay and Kaleva. Some bought old farms; eighty acres with a few buildings, a tractor, a flock of chickens and maybe a cow could be purchased for $7000. Others camped in plastic lean-tos, teepees or abandoned saunas.

The newcomers stuck to themselves, coming into town every couple of weeks to pick up their mail and shop at the co-op store where most had their only contact with what they referred to as "real Sointula people." While the early Finns had advertized their utopia in the *Aika*, rumours of a hippie commune rippled down the coast by word of mouth. There was a lot of coming and going, creating the impression that there was a larger counter-culture population on the island than there actually was.

As well as offering sanctuary from the United States draft and the lure of cheap land, Canada was also attractive for its socialized medical care. A trip to Sointula to visit some friends convinced Kit and Stephanie Eakle to have their baby in British Columbia. They moved to Malcolm Island from Cal-

A traditional Finnish home on Kaleva Road, 1978. (Rick James)

Old Tom, the communist logger, lectures a hippie on "the dignity of the working man," 1974. The light bulb over the door indicated whether the Variety Store was open or closed. (Rick James)

ifornia in May 1970, and at the end of the summer they were asked to caretake Jane and John McClendon's place. In 1969 the McClendons had bought an old homestead which they used first as a summer home and later as a permanent residence. Their Kaleva farm was a destination point for a lot of the hippies, many believing that it was the site of an active commune. While that was not true, Jane did let people sleep on the farmhouse floor or in one of the outbuildings.

"People called Jane 'Mom' because she was a little bit older than the rest of us and she fed everyone," Stephanie said. "When Kit and I were caretaking their place, we felt obliged to continue that tradition. People would show up with two pounds of brown rice and ask to stay indefinitely. We were all city people and didn't really know much about living off the land."

The Eakles decided to have their baby at "home," an old sauna at McClendon's that had been converted into a cabin, rather than the hospital in Alert Bay. Other pregnant women were invited, Stephanie's parents came from California, and a sister arrived from New York. An ex-Vietnam medic promised to oversee the delivery but showed up two months late. "It was really exciting until complications set in and my parents had to charter a float plane to take me to Alert Bay," Stephanie recalled. "There was no ambulance on the island in those days and we weren't connected enough with the locals to know anyone with a fishing boat."

In fact, the hippies' connections with the locals were varied. Many of the older generation of Finns were open and friendly. They looked beyond the long hair and strange clothes and saw people who wanted a simple lifestyle, whose dreams echoed their parents' ideals. They observed the newcomers buying the farms that their children had abandoned and watched while they cleared fields of timothy and wild grasses, repaired broken fences and windows and removed the rubble left from rambunctious teenagers dynamiting chimneys.

Willie Olney noted: "The hippie movement gave Sointula a complete freedom of fashion. They wore weird get-ups but they looked so comfortable. Pretty soon it seemed like everyone could wear whatever they wanted. Before the hippies came women wore nylons all the time. People die in the winter and most of our funerals are outside. Women used to freeze in the wind and rain but after the hippies were here for awhile it was acceptable to wear pants."

While most of the older residents were accepting, their children were suspicious and sometimes hostile. They had worked hard to improve their lives and found it difficult to understand these strangers who turned their backs on the modern conveniences of life. To compound the matter, none of the new people seemed to have jobs, a fact that irritated and puzzled the hard-working Finns. Also, although only a small percentage of the hippies were draft dodgers, the locals believed otherwise. Many of the middle-aged men, more patriotic than pro-Vietnam, viewed the newcomers as cowards who wouldn't fight for their country. And then there were the rumours about drugs and free love.

"We felt frightened when the hippies came," Bonnie Nelson admitted. "We had to start locking our doors, we had heard stories about people going crazy on drugs. It seemed like there were a lot of them and everyone felt that life would change because of them."

"Life did change when the hippies came," Aileen Wooldridge stated. "Up until that time everybody knew each other and most people were related in some way. We were a tight-knit little community and all of a sudden there were all these other people. It couldn't stay the same. There was a lot of resentment because things were changing."

The youth of the island, in the rebellious years of their teens and early twenties, were openly curious about and even attracted to the hippies. Their interest further increased the tension between their parents and the "long hairs," who were held responsible for the drugs that were beginning to appear on the island.

"After we had been in Sointula for awhile I screwed up enough courage to go to Granny's Cafe," Jenny reminisced. "I sat there for twenty minutes and was ignored—they wouldn't serve me. For the first time in my life I knew what it was like to be a minority. A few days later though, I was walking down the street and there was this older Finn man walking towards me. I smiled at him and his face just opened up in the most beautiful smile. I realized then that some of the problem was my own shyness and insecurity."

Other reactions to the hippies were more aggressive. There was talk of running them out of town. Local logging truck drivers played chicken with hippie vehicles travelling to Mitchell Bay, and a truck that broke down on the logging road was torched.

Jimmy "Slim" Erickson, of Finnish descent, has coffee at Granny's Cafe with Windsor, Ontario expatriate Walter Miller and son Devin, January 1976. (Rick James)

In the summer of 1971 an old cellar on Kaleva Road, home to an ever-changing group of hippies, was the site of a pre-dawn drug raid. Rumour had it that the RCMP found LSD hidden in the wood pile but chose to let the prime suspect escape. A few weeks later the cellar burned to the ground. No one was living there at the time and, although no charges were ever laid, most hippies believed that the fire was deliberately set by locals.

While members of the counter-culture felt that some Malcolm Islanders were not friendly, they did not necessarily expect them to be and were satisfied as long as the hostilities didn't get out of control. Stephanie reflected: "We felt that the town was not friendly but we weren't either. We were raised in the city and didn't expect people to care about who we were. But the Finns were curious about us and some did want to

The Geisreiters liked the look of what was going to be the barn so much that they made it their house instead. Wood for the house was obtained from their property and the beach as well as the mill at Telegraph Cove. There were no nails used in the house; all the wood was notched and pinioned. (Geisreiter collection)

be friends. I'm sure we alienated some of them with our attitudes."

Not all the newcomers to the island were hippies. There were others, a little older and with children of their own, who longed to return to the basic values of an earlier time. Mendicino, California residents Dick and Bette Geisreiter bought the eighty-five acre Halminen farm in 1968 and moved to the island two years later. "It was the era when people were going back to the land," Bette said. "We were burned out from working so hard and were looking for a slower lifestyle. All of our relatives thought we had lost our marbles, but really we had found them. The wonderful thing about Sointula was the simplicity, it was another age. When we got off the ferry a lot of people were there, including a woman wearing a big Mexican hat. Years later I found out that Doris Siider had heard that there were people from California on the boat and had worn that hat to make us feel at home."

Like the Tynjalas who moved from North Dakota in 1902, the Geisreiters brought all their worldly possessions with them. Their caravan included five cars, a Volkswagen van converted into a chuck wagon, an old telephone van and a one-ton truck filled with tools and windows for the house they were building. Accompanying the couple were their three sons, friends to drive all the vehicles, Zeke the dog, plus thirteen goats with six kids. Bette said, "We picked the best stock to

Dick and Bette Geisreiter and their sons, Billie and John, begin a new life on Malcolm Island, 1970. (Geisreiter collection)

take with us. To get the goats into Canada Dick had to dip them in a sulphur solution. I guess that sterilized their skin, it sure turned them a nice lime green."

Everyone that moved to the island attempted to live a self-sufficient lifestyle. Most chopped their own firewood, planted large gardens and canned their surplus produce. "At that time getting back to the land was the Mecca we all said we wanted," one person noted. "Living in Mitchell Bay, we didn't have much choice, that's pretty well all there was."

The Geisreiters however were serious about their lifestyle change. "One of our goals was to do as little shopping as possible," Bette remembered. "We grew most of our own food and were self-sustaining to eighty percent. We sold vegetables and cheese to the co-op. We also had a milk route and sold milk, butter, and eggs. We shopped at the co-op once a week and every couple of months Dick would go to Vancouver and fill the back of the truck with a couple hundred pounds of flour, sugar, and other staples."

The Geisreiters and others like them found that hard work and perseverance paid off in more than just personal satisfaction; it earned them the respect and friendship of the islanders. For many, music was the key that opened doors. "We'd go to Lempi and John Blid's for a sauna and then the gang would come over and we'd play music until 2:00 or 3:00 in the morning," Dick said. "There was a mandolin, a banjo, an accordion and sometimes a piano. We played at weddings, funerals and anniversaries. It was a fun way to mix with the community."

Although many of the people coming to Malcolm Island were talented, it was soon apparent that backgrounds in Chinese studies, economics and floral design were not particularly useful in their new home. Just as the early tailors and poets struggled to fell trees and operate a sawmill, so the newcomers had to adapt their urban skills to a rural environment. They met the challenge with a combination of hope and confidence, and even those without any practical experience never doubted that they could build a house and live off the land.

The Soltaus moved to Sointula in 1971 after an abortive attempt to go back to the land in Kansas. They were looking for "a hippie haven, an untapped wilderness, where the government was giving away free (Crown) land." With the Eakles, they bought fifty-four acres near the lighthouse at Pulteney Point and in 1972 moved there with their two-year-old daughter and one-month-old son. Home was an army tent with an airtight heater.

"It seemed like an adventure at the time," Heidi said. "I had blind faith in Will's ability to build a house—he had studied architecture and built some chairs."

"I wasn't really prepared to go back to the land," Will admitted. "I'd always lived in the suburbs. I had some drafting experience, a couple of books and a little generator to run a few power tools. A lot of the house was built with a chain saw."

The two families attempted to limit their purchases to staples like oil and salt. They caught fish, baked

Will and Heidi Soltau in front of their army tent home at Pulteney Point, 1972. Their airtight stove was multi-purpose: it provided heat, sterilized baby bottles and was the kitchen stove. (Soltau collection)

bread, raised chickens and goats and always ate their evening meal together. Even after they had built separate homes, dinners remained a communal effort. Roughing it in the 1970s wasn't much easier than it had been at the turn of the century. Heidi's Pulteney Point memories revolve around wet fire wood and crying while she milked the goats because her hands had cramped with the cold. She cooked meals and sterilized baby bottles on the airtight stove and remembers the day the goats broke into the tent and took one bite out of each potato.

Sooner or later the newcomers' dream of living off the land gave way to the reality of having to earn a living. Some found employment on government-funded Local Initiatives Programs making street signs, cleaning senior's yards and landscaping the hall hill (where they were frequently accused of smoking marijuana behind the hall), but the real money was to be made in the logging and fishing industries. Scrambling through the bush and over windfalls, the philosophy graduate learned to set chokers while the weaver mastered the intricacies of mending a seine net. A side benefit to the on-the-job training were the horror stories about accidents and death, widow makers and snapped beach lines. Jobs for men were plentiful but there wasn't much in the way of work for women.

Jane McClendon moved to the island permanently in 1972. "Unless you were part of a family with a fish boat, women usually didn't get fishing jobs. So around 1974 I started a tree planting co-op." An island dump fire that got out of (control was Jane's first planting contract. She could only find five experienced planters so she and a few others trained forty more. A core group of twenty newcomers bought shares of $50 and formed the tree planting co-op Treesing. Half of the membership had to be women and all members had to be Malcolm Island residents. Contracts were run on a cooperative basis; on many jobs the crew lived and ate together, often camping in tents and lean-tos.

At first positions on the board of directors were filled by

Treesing, tree planting co-operative, at work in the snow at Frederick Arm, November 1975. Standing left to right: Simon Dick, Janey Lord, Stewart Marshall, Kathy Gibler, Edda Field, Barb Imlach, Ralph Harris, Mike Field, Anthea Cameron. Sitting: Sid Williams and Robbie Boyes. Treesing was formed in 1974 to provide jobs for newcomers to Malcolm Island, particularly women. (Rick James)

women but one by one they found other jobs and the nature of the co-op began to change. As more co-op members moved on to other things it became necessary to hire people from off island. Originally a true co-op with no paid management, a new, all-male board of directors decided that they should be compensated for their responsibilities. On the verge of becoming a business rather than a co-op, Treesing dissolved in 1988.

Before they became involved with Treesing, Kathy Gibler and Anthea Cameron established their own work protection plan. One summer they decided to apply for fishing jobs but on their way to the dock realized that they would be lucky if there was a job for one woman let alone two. They

Danni Tribe using today's aluminum version of Laurie Jarvis' gillnet drum on the north shore of Malcolm Island, 1987. (Paula Wild)

agreed that whoever got the job would split her income with the other.

"Anthea got the job," Kathy said. "Later that week I got a job fertilizing trees for a forestry crew. We ran around with big flour sifters on our backs which spit out stuff that looked like coarse salt. Anthea and I both worked for three days. At the end of that time she gave me $300 and I gave her $75. We kept that up for over a year. We weren't living in the same house but it seemed like a good plan."

In another communal effort, newcomers to the island joined a Vancouver-based food co-op called Movable Feast. An order book was passed around and volunteers compiled a master list pooling everyone's hulk orders. "Someone would take a truck down to Vancouver, work in the co-op warehouse for a few days, then bring the order up island," Ralph Harris remembered. "A lot of our basics were provided for that way. The Sointula Co-op didn't carry things that we wanted, like wheat germ, nutritional yeast and soya sauce."

As well as working and purchasing items cooperatively, most of the newcomers became close friends. Sharlene and Roger Sommer and their three children moved to Sointula from Sacramento, California, in June 1970. "Roger was an accountant and I was a housewife who stayed home and looked after the kids," Sharlene explained. "When I first saw the hippies in Sointula I was scared of them, but eventually I became friends with them because most of them were American. Our

Granny Jarvis, the wife of gillnet drum inventor Laurie Jarvis, was born in the Klondike during the height of the gold rush. Here she is taking a closer look at Rob Wynne and Doug, two recent arrivals to the island, 1974. (Rick James)

Davey and Les Lanqvist keep an eye on the fish tally as the seine boat *Millionaires* is unloaded at Sointula's Norpac barge, July 1977. Many newcomers to the island broke into the fishing industry on the *Millionaires*. (Rick James)

first Thanksgiving in Sointula I was in tears because I had never been away from my family. All the Americans felt that way to some extent, so we all baked bread and killed our own turkeys or chickens and got together for a big meal. I realized then that family isn't necessarily blood."

But even those who weren't classed as hippies ran into problems with the locals. The first incident occurred in 1968 when a Finn demanded more money from a Californian who had bought his farm. The two men were arguing in the kitchen when one of them grabbed a rifle. There was a struggle, the gun went off and the Finn was shot. Not having a telephone or a car, the American ran to a neighbour's for help and ended up driving the injured man into town on his tractor. In the interim the Finn bled to death. This incident upset the newcomers more than the longtime residents. As an American living on the island at the time, Jenny felt that, "people looked at us a bit after that but we didn't really feel like they held it against us as a group until a different American closed the logging road. That really created a lot of hard feelings, more so than the shooting."

When Roger and Sharlene bought their farm it included an access road linking Sointula to the small community and log dump at Mitchell Bay. Everyone used this road, including the local logging company which paid a nominal fee to do so. When the lease expired, Roger increased the fee, hoping that the loggers would find another route. The logging company balked, negotiations broke down, and Roger barricaded the road. A lot of yelling took place, there were threats of physical violence and rocks were thrown at the Sommers' house. Once when Roger went to Mitchell Bay to visit friends the road was blocked so he couldn't get home. When, in spite of the harassment, Roger refused to change his mind the "dump" road was extended to become the new link between Mitchell Bay and Sointula.

By the mid-1970s the Finns' hard edges of suspicion and protectiveness had been worn thin by familiarity. Arriving in Sointula via Port McNeill, Vancouver and Detroit, Mary Murphy said: "The people in Sointula were more friendly than any place else I had ever lived. In the city everyone distrusts everyone else, but here people offer you rides and are curious about what you are doing. I was pregnant and everyone seemed interested in my health and the baby. I got the feeling that the locals approved of us because we had a garden and were starting a family."

"There was a difference after I worked in the co-op store," Mary continued. "Here you need to show that you are a hard worker to be accepted. Work is more than just a job, it's almost a community activity."

Over the years most of the hippies traded their long hair for more conventional styles and became involved in the routines that owning a home and raising a family bring. An interest and concern about what was happening found them attending community meetings and volunteering for committees. Although there is still some vestiges of "them" and "us," for the most part the newcomers have been accepted. As one Finn said, "They've become such a part of the island that I can't imagine it without them. Besides, they're not really hippies anymore."

CHAPTER SIXTEEN

The Paradox of Change

TODAY APPROXIMATELY 750 PEOPLE MAKE THEIR home on Malcolm Island. In the spring the streets are lined with the vivid reds and yellows of Scotch broom, while honeysuckle and wild roses climb sheds and fences bleached gray by the sun. On a warm day the sweet scent of the cottonwood tree on the Pink property fills the air. Finnish can still be heard on the streets and in the co-op store and much of the spoken English has a distinctly Finnish inflection. Time is measured by the coming and going of the ferry rather than the passing of hours.

A short walk from the hotel, ferry and post office, the Sointula Co-op is located in the heart of "town." One of the oldest continuing consumer's cooperatives in North America, the imposing, stucco building is the pulse of the island, a place to catch up on local news as well as buy groceries. A few blocks away on the hill overlooking the main street, an enlarged Finnish Organization Hall continues to be used for meetings, funerals, dances and weddings.

It has been estimated that close to 2000 people came to Malcolm Island during the four-year span of the Kalevan Kansa. The Finnish immigrants working in Nanaimo's coal mines at the turn of the century possessed the physical strength and *sisu* to create Sointula on their own, but they wanted the "eloquence and sharp pen" of Matti Kurikka to promote their ideas. While Kurikka's flamboyance and charisma drew the

Anderson Marine Ways, 1974. Anderson Marine Ways, the first of Sointula's nine boat yards, was established in 1918. Although the shop no
longer builds boats, it still does repairs and continues to be run by the
Anderson family. The house in the background was the original colony
cabin. (Rick James)

settlers to Sointula, it was the practical, down-to-earth Marxist Mäkelä that the colonists relied on when the Kalevan Kama
collapsed. Even after their dreams of utopia had slipped away,
the Finns held fast to their desire to create, or at least direct,
their own destiny. For over forty years they based their society on a system of cooperative efforts, creating a legacy of
independent self-reliance that is still alive today.

In the past Malcolm Islanders were united by their
language, heritage, ideals and pride in their community. For
much of its history Sointula was more Finnish than Canadian,
but regular ferry runs have made the island accessible as a
bedroom community for northern Vancouver Island and as a

summer retreat for urban centres. Amenities now include two convenience stores, two churches, a liquor agency, a licensed hotel and an RCMP substation. Names like Miller, Hamilton and Jones are as common as Huopalainen, Wirkki and Syr-jala.

The paradox of change is readily visible. Large, new homes are patterned on suburban subdivisions rather than the small but sturdy Finnish or funky hippy dwellings, and half-a-dozen bed and breakfasts and a couple of fishing lodges cater to tourists, who in the not-so-distant past were discouraged from visiting the island. In quaint contrast, cedar boat sheds lean precariously with age, and some of the houses and yards, once renowned for their immaculate European neatness, present peeling paint, dilapidated fences and over-grown gardens. Even the locals admit that people don't cut their lawns as often as they used to and that the island is not as tidy as it once was.

Malcolm Island's isolated location and the barrier of the Finnish language made it easy for the Finns to preserve their distinct culture. But access to the outside world and the passing of the original pioneers have weakened these insular boundaries. Prosperity has replaced the need to rely on others; adversity is no longer faced as a collective unit. For now Sointula's Finnish and utopian roots provide a link with the past, but that unique sense of community spirit is fading with each generation.

Above: Janet and Ted (Teuvo) Tanner, 1993. Ted's father, Theodore, was one of the founding members of the Kalevan Kansa and one of the first Finns to arrive on Malcolm Island in 1901. Janet's family moved to Sointula in 1925 after her father met people from Sointula at a Russian commune near the Sea of Azov. (Rick James)

Below: Weekend net mending for the crews of seine boats *Star Tania* and *Maple Leaf C*. Mark Homer, Paul Bozenich, Larry Sjoberg, Larry "Snuffy" Holmes and Karl "Smug" Souch, July 1982. (Rick James)

One of the most prosperous fishing fleets on the west coast ties up at the Sointula breakwater for the winter, 1977. (Rick James)

Looking down First Street from the hall hill on a winter day, February 1979. (Rick James)

Above: Sointula seiners "anchored out on the spot"; Barkley Sound, June 1983. Left to right: John Cameron, Ross Michelson, Jamie Erickson, Larry Sjoberg, Bob —, Donna Anderson. (Rick James)
Below: Christine Wynne mending nets, 1975. Like many newcomers to the island, Chris held a variety of jobs. In addition to mending nets she also worked on her brother Rob's garbage truck and was bookkeeper/teller at the Sointula Credit Union. (Rick James)

Charlie Peterson and Johnny Malm, 1976. When Charlie moved to Sointula in 1922 he claimed to be "the first white man on the island. Before
I came there were only Finns and Indians here." Charlie married Sally,
the daughter of Finnish pioneer Theodore Tanner. Johnny is the third
generation of Malms to live on Malcolm Island. (Rick James)

When the second Sointula Co-op store became too small, this two-and-a-
half-story building was built in 1953. (SC)

An excerpt from the agreement between the provincial government and the Kalevan Kansa Colonization Company, signed on November 29, 1901:

1) The Kalevan Kansa is to obtain free ownership of Malcolm Island in the Rupert District of British Columbia for the purpose of establishing a settlement under the following proposals and conditions.

2) The Kalevan Kansa agrees to undertake the amount of improvements required under the Land Grant Act, which amount to $2.50 per acre for the area of approximately 28,000 acres.

3) From the beginning of this contract the Kalevan Kansa shall for the next seven years be free from all provincial taxation with the exception of the $3.00 per person Revenue Tax. On its own, and without the assistance of the government, the Kalevan Kansa must complete all public works which the residents will need: roads, bridges, and public buildings, with the exception of schools and wharves.

4) The Kalevan Kama will not receive the deed to the island or to any part of it until seven years from this day, and until the Minister of Lands and Labour has been given sufficient proof that 350 men (one for each 80 acres) have been located on the island, and that all the stipulations of this agreement have been fully complied with.

5) The roads, streets, bridges, and public buildings, and wharves, which the Kalevan Kansa undertakes to erect, or to have built, must be constructed under the supervision and control of the Minister of Lands and Labour, and the size of individual allotments of land and their order of distribution also requires the approval of the Minister of Lands and Labour.

6) All the Kalevan Kansa's improvement projects must meet the satisfaction of the Minister of Lands and Labour, and the improvements must in total equal $2.50 per acre for the

island's 28,000 acres.

7) The Kalevan Kansa shall establish a settler or head of household for each 80 acres on Malcolm Island.

8) Every member who settles on the island as a permanent resident will be required to obtain British citizenship.

9) Children beyond grade two of elementary school must attend an English language school.

10) If the Kalevan Kansa is successful the government will grant another tract of land similar in size and as near Malcolm Island as possible.

An excerpt from the financial report from the Kalevan Kansa Colonization Company annual general meeting read at the Juhannus Celebration in Sointula June 1902:

Prior to the fifteenth of this month, membership dues totaled $3,313.60 and an additional $150.00 has been raised by selling shares in the *Aika* newspaper. Donations of $114.45 have been received, and of that $108.95 has been appropriated for the piano fund, and $4.00 for the immigration assistance fund. Additional sources of income equal $3.00. The *Aika* Printing Company has been awarded a loan of $200.00 which is to be used to straighten out the debts incurred by the newspaper.

Expenses for establishment costs, travelling expenses, etc., have been $380.00; money for machinery and equipment, boats, vessels maintenance and fitting, dishes and other furnishings total $1,388.90; clothing and shoes $410.90; food $1,019.40; wages $250.00; printing costs $100.00; medicine $3.50; and rent $3.50.

Money in hand totals $174.55 plus $150.00 for shares in the *Aika*. For machinery and equipment the Kalevan Kansa has a debt of approximately $600.00; for food and clothing approximately $400.00, which along with a loan of $300.00 to construct living quarters, creates a debt of $1,300.00 not withstanding the wages due to the company's own members.

The board of directors elected for the Kalevan Kansa Colonization Company at Sointula in June 1902:

Matti Kurikka, President
Oswald Beckman, Vice-president and Manager
Austin Mäkelä, Secretary
Victor Jalo, Assistant Secretary
August Oberg, Treasurer and Project Organizer
Alfred Ruis, Labour Organizer
V. Karstunen, Stock Keeper
Richard Puro, Auditor
Andrew Willander and J. H. Tonsk, Assistant Auditors
Malakias Kyto
H. Lukkarinen
G. Iron
Theodore Tanner
V. Vesa
Andrew Aho
Matti Halminen

While the vice-president, secretary, treasurer and manager were appointed by the board, the president was elected by a majority of the colonists. The vote for Matti Kurikka was unanimous.

PEOPLE:

Interviews by author:

Andy Barlak. Sointula, 1988.
Alf Bayne. Quadra Island, 1993.
John Beckman. Sointula,1988.
Kay Briggs. Sointula,1988.
Laila Butcher. Burnaby, 1993.
Stephanie Eakle. Sointula, 1988.
Warren Ekness. Sointula,1988.
Jane Field. Sointula,1988.
Mary Anne Foster. Sointula,1992.
Dick & Bette Geisreiter. Victoria, 1989.
Kathy Gibler. Sointula, 1989.
Jenny Green. Victoria, 1992.
Ralph Harris. Mitchell Bay, 1988.
Emily Hilton. New Westminster, 1993.
Diane Hufnagel. Sointula, 1988.
Rick James. Fanny Bay, 1988.
Virginia Macfarlane. Portland, Oregon, 1988.
Mary Murphy. Sointula,1988.
Bonnie Nelson. Sointula, 1988.
Willie Olney. Sointula, 1988.
Meralda Pink. Sointula, 1992.
Loretta Rihtamo. Sointula, 1988.
Tauno Salo. Sointula, 1988.
Heidi Soltau. Sointula, 1988.
Will Soltau. Sointula,1992.
Roger Sommer. Courtenay, 1993.
Sharlene Sommer. Sointula, 1992.
Carol Sommers. Sointula, 1992.
Ted & Janet Tanner. Sointula,1992.
Danni Tribe. Sointula, 1992.
Dick Weyer. Sointula,1993.
Aileen Wooldridge. Sointula, 1993.
Sylvia Yoneda. Fort Bragg, California, 1993.

CONVERSATIONS:

David Hunt, Chief, Fort Rupert Kwakiutl Band. Sept. 1985.
Matti Linnoila, great-grandson of Matti Kurikka. Sointula 1988.
Peter MacNair, Ethnologist, Royal B.C. Museum. July 1992.

ORAL HISTORY TAPES:

Homer, Wayne/Fish, Gordon. British Columbia Archives and Records Service. Victoria. Call No. 4031:26.
Kilboume, Charles/Noble, Jim. December 1978. Sointula Museum.
Maki, Sam/Fish, Gordon. British Columbia Archives and Records Service. Victoria. Call No. 4031:40.
Michelson, Dickie/Fish, Gordon. British Columbia Archives and Records Service. Victoria. Call No. 4031:32–33.
Michelson, Irene/Fish, Gordon. British Columbia Archives and Records Service. Victoria. Call No. 4031:25.
Michelson, Richard/Langlois, John. Vancouver Cultural Communities Series Oral History Project. Interview Number 64.
Oksanen, Vilho/Fish, Gordon. British Columbia Archives and Records Service. Victoria. Call No. 4031:14.
Peterson, Sally & Charlic/Fish, Gordon. British Columbia Arehives and Records Service. Victoria. Call No. 4031:21–22.
Pouttu, Alex/Fish, Gordon. British Columbia Archives and Records Service. Victoria. Call No. 3041 :23.
Riksman, Katri (trans. Edith Cadorin)/Orchard, Imbert. British Columbia Archives and Records Service. Victoria. Call No. 1017:1.
Tanner, Janet and Ted/Fish, Gordon. British Columbia Archives and Records Service. Victoria. Call No. 4031:30 & 31.
Tynjala, Arvo/Kennedy, Murray. British Columbia Archives and Records Service. Call No. 1016–2 & 3.
Tynjala, Arvo/Orchard, Imbert. British Columbia Archives and Records Service. Victoria. Call No. 1016–5.
Tynjala, Urho/Kennedy, Munay. British Columbia Archives and Records Service. Victoria. Call No. 74:1.

Williams, Alfred B./ Anderson, Olaivi J./Fish, Gordon.
British Columbia Archives and Records Service. Victoria.
Call No. 4031:38–40.

BOOKS:

Anderson, Doris. *Evergreen Islands, The Islands of the
Inside Passage: Quadra to Malcolm*. Sidney, British
Columbia: Gray's Publishing Ltd., 1979.
Avakumovic, Ivan. *The Communist Party in Canada, A
History*. Toronto: McClelland and Stewart Limited, 1975.
Bergren, Myrtle Woodward. *Tough Timber: The Loggers of
B.C., Their Story*. Vancouver: Elgrin Publishers, 1979.
Boam, Henry J. *British Columbia: Its History, People,
Commerce and Resources*. London: Sells Ltd., 1912.
Boas, Franz. *Ethnology of the Kwakiutl: Based on Data
Collected by Franz Boas and George Hunt. Volume I*. 35th
Annual Report of the Bureau of American Ethnology to
the Secretary of the Smithsonian Institution. Washington:
1921.
Boas, Franz. *Geographical Names of the Kwakiutl Indians*.
New York: Columbia University Press, 1934.
Boas, Franz. *Kwakiutl Culture as Reflected in Mythology*.
New York: The American Folk-Lore Society, 1935.
Boas, Franz. *Kwakiutl Tales Volume II*. New York: Columbia
University Press, 1910.
Boas, Franz and Hunt, George. *The Jessup North Pacific
Expedition, Memoir of the American Museum of Natural
History, New York, Volume III, Kwakiutl Texts*. ed. Franz
Boas. New York: G.E. Stechert, 1905.
Boas, Franz and Hunt, George. *The Jessup North Pacific
Expedition, Memoir of the American Museum of Natural
History, New York, Volume X, Kwakiutl Texts*. New York:
G.E. Stechert, 1906.
Bowen, Lynne. *Boss Whistle: The Coal Miners of Vancouver
Island Remember*. Lantzville, British Columbia: Oolichan
Books, 1982.
British Columbia Directory. 1895. British Columbia
Archives.

Eklund, William. *Builders of Canada: History of the Finnish Organization of Canada*, 1911–1971. Finnish Organization of Canada, 1987.

Fish, Gordon and Lillard, Charles, eds. *Dreams of Freedom: Bella Coola, Cape Scott, Sointula*. Victoria: Sound Heritage Series, 1982.

Forester, Joseph E. and Anne D. *British Columbia's Commercial Fishing History*. Surrey: Hancock House, 1975.

Hall, Wendy. *Green Gold and Granite: A Background to Finland*. London: Parrish, 1953.

Halminen, Matti. *Sointula, Kalevan Kansan ja Kanadan Süomalaisten Historiaa. (The History of Sointula and the Kalevan Kansa)*. Helsinki, Finland: Mikko Ampuja Kustantaja, 1936. Translated by Allan Henry Salo.

Hannula, Reino. *Blueberry God: The Education of a Finnish-American*. San Louis Obispo: Quality Hill, 1979.

Hill, A.V. *Tides of Change, the Story of Fishermen's Co-operatives in British Columbia*. Prince Rupert: Prince Rupert Fishermen's Co-operative Association, 1967.

Hill, Beth and Ray. *Indian Petrogylphs of the Pacific Northwest*. Saanichton, B.C.: Hancock House, 1974.

Hoglund, A. William. *Finnish Immigrants in America 1880–1920*. Madison, Wisconsin: University of Wisconsin Press, 1960.

Jääskeläinen, Kaapro (A.B. Mäkelä). *Muistoja Malkosaarelta (Memoirs of Malcolm Island)*. Helsinki: Työväen Kirjapaino, 1907. Selected translations by Anja Auer, Tauno Salo, Janet and Ted Tanner, Loretta Rihtamo, and Tuula Lewis.

Jalkanen, Ralph J., ed. *The Finns in North America: A Social Symposium*. Hancock, Michigan: Michigan State University, 1969.

Kalemaa, Kalevi. *Matti Kurikka, Legendajo Elaessaan (A Legend In His Own Lifetime)*. Finland: Juva Werner Soderström Osakeyhtiö, 1978. Selected translations by Tuula Lewis.

Kanter, Rosabeth, M. *Commitment & Community, Communes and Utopias in a Sociological Perspective*. Cambridge, Massachusetts: Harvard University Press, 1972.

Koivukangas, Olavi. *Sea, Gold and Sugarcane, Finns in Australia 1851–1947*. Turku, Finland: Institute of Migration, 1986.

Lyons, Cicely. *Salmon: Our Heritage, The Story of a Province and an Industry*. Vancouver: British Columbia Packers Limited, 1969.

Manuel, Frank E. *Utopias and Utopian Thought*. Boston: Houghton Mifflin Company and The American Academy of Arts and Sciences, 1966.

Meggs, Geoff. *Salmon, The Decline of the British Columbia Fishery*. Vancouver/Toronto: Douglas & McIntyre, 1991.

More, Thomas. *Utopia*. ed. by Surtz, S.J. London: Yale University Press, 1964.

Nikols, Sheila, Bokstrom, Violet, MacDonald, Isabelle, Mussallem, Grace, Sleigh, Daphne, Smith, Margaret. *Maple Ridge: A History of Settlement*. British Columbia: Maple Ridge Branch, Canadian Federation of University Women, 1972.

Norcross, E. Blanche, ed. *The Company on the Coast*. Nanaimo: Nanaimo Historical Society, 1983.

Norris, John. *Strangers Entertained: A History of the Ethnic Groups of British Columbia*. Vancouver: Evergreen Press, 1971.

Peltoniemi, Teuvo. *"Sointula, B.C. Kurikkalaisten Malkosaari."* (Sointula and Kurikka). Kohti Parempaa Maailmaa. Ottawa, 1985. Select translations by Tuula Lewis, Loretta Rihtamo, Tauno (and Ruth) Salo and Janet and Ted Tanner.

Sargent, Lyman Tower. *Contemporary Political Ideologies, A Comparative Analysis*. St. Louis: University of Missouri, 1975.

Speck, Dara Culhane. *An Error in Judgment, The Politics of Medical Care in an Indian/White Community*. Vancouver: Talonbooks,1987.

Viherjuuri, H. J. Sauna: *The Finnish Bath*. Vermont: Stephen Greene Press, 1972.

Walbran, Captain John T. *British Columbia Coast Names*. Vancouver: Douglas and McIntyre, 1971.

Wuorinen, J.H. *The History of Finland*. New York: Columbia University Press, 1965.

PAMPHLETS:

Anderson, Aili and Tynjala, Aini. *History of Sointula*. Vancouver: Sointula Centennial Committee, 1958.

Laine, Ed. Public Archives of Canada. Selections from the Finnish Organization of Canada Collection.

Lindstrom-Best, Varpu. *The Finns in Canada*. Ottawa: The Canadian Historical Society, 1985.

Mertanen, P. and Eklund, W. *The Illegal Finnish Organization of Canada Inc*. Ontario: Vapaus Publishing Co., June 1942.

North Island Heritage Inventory & Evaluation, Regional District of Mount Waddington. British Columbia, 1984.

PUBLISHED ARTICLES:

Ampuja, Mikko. "Matti Halminen, Sointulan Historian Kirjoittaja." (Matti Halminen, Sointula Historian). *Demokraattisen Kansan Kalenteri*. Helsinki, 1948. Translated by Tuula Lewis.

Eklund, William. "The Formative Years of the Finnish Organization of Canada." *Finnish Diaspora 1: Canada, South American, Africa, Australia and Sweden*. ed. Karni, Michael G. Toronto: The Multicultural History Society of Ontario, 1981.

Garber-Conrad, Beckle. "Sointula Co-op—1909." Cooperative Consumer. February 1978. Sointula Museum.

Gough, Barry M. "Fort Rupert, Its Coal and Its Spar Trades." *The Company on the Coast*. ed. Norcross, E. Blanche. The Nanaimo Historical Society. 1983.

Graham, Donald. *Lights of the Inside Passage. A History of British Columbia Lighthouses and Their Keepers*. Madeira Park: Harbour Publishing, 1986.

Gross, Richard. "Sointula: Home of the Gillnet Drum." *The Westcoast Fisherman*, Vancouver: March 1988: 17–20.

Kajanus-Blenner, Lilly. "My Uncle Matti Kurikka." Translated by Tuula Lewis. Sointula Museum.

Kero, Reino. "The Canadian Finns in Soviet Karelia in the
1930s." *Finnish Diaspora I: Canada, South American,
Africa, Australia and Sweden*. ed. Karni, Michael G.
Toronto: The Multicultural History Society of Ontario,
1981.

Koivukangas,Olavi. "An Attempted Finnish Utopian
Settlement in Queensland." *Journal of the Royal
Australian Historical Society, Vol. 58*. (March 1972).

Kolemainen, John. "Harmony Island: A Finnish Utopian
Venture in B.C." *British Columbia Historical Quarterly
#5*. Victoria, B.C.: Archives of British Columbia in co-
operation with the B.C. Historical Foundation, 1941.

Lahti, Osmo. *Finnish Canadian Miners in North Wellington,
Nanaimo, Extension and Ladysmith, British Columbia*.
The Nanaimo Historical Society. Vancouver: 1989.

Laine, Edward, W. "Finnish Canadian Radicalism and
Canadian Politics: The First Forty Years, 1900–1940."
Ethnicity, Power and Politics in Canada, Vol. VIII,
Canadian Ethnic Studies Association. ed. Jorgen Dahlie
and Tissa Fernando. Toronto: Methuen, 1981.

Lindstrom-Best, Varpu. "The Socialist Party of Canada and
the Finnish Connection, 1905–1911." *Ethnicity, Power and
Politics in Canada, Vol. VIII*, Canadian Ethnic Studies
Association. ed. Jorgen Dahlie and Tissa Fernando.
Toronto: Methuen, 1981.

"Sammon Takojat." *Men on the Fraser River—Socialist
Dreamers*. Translated by Violet Bokstrom. Maple Ridge
Museum.

Peltoniemi, Teuvo. "Sointula, B.C. Kurikkalaisten
Malkosaari." (Kurikka in Sointula, B.C.) *Kohti Parempaa
Maailmaa*. Ottawa: 1985. Select translations by Tuula
Lewis, Anja Auer and Violet Bokstrom.

Pilli, Arja. "Finnish-Canadian Radicalism and the
Government of Canada from the First World War to
the Depression." *Finnish Diaspora I: Canada, South
American, Africa, Australia and Sweden*. ed. Michael
G. Kami. Toronto: The Multicultural History Society of
Ontario, 1981.

Wilson, J. Donald. "Matti Kurikka: Finnish-Canadian
Intellectual." *B.C. Studies*, (Winter 1973–74): 50–65.

Wilson, J. Donald. "A Synoptic View of the *Aika*, Canada's First Finnish Language Newspaper." *Amphora, No. 29* (March 1980).

Wilson, J. Donald "Never Believe What You Have Never Doubted, Matti Kurikka's Dream for a New World Utopia." *Finnish Diaspora 1, Canada, South American, Africa, Australia and Sweden*. ed. Michael G. Karni. Toronto: The Multicultural History Society of Ontario, 1981.

Wilson, Donald J. "Matti Kurikka and A. B. Mäkelä: Socialist Thought Among Finns In Canada." *Canadian Ethnic Studies Vol. X*, no. 2 (1978): 9–21.

Woodcock, George. "Harmony Island: A Canadian Utopia." *British Columbia: A Centennial Anthology*. ed. Watters, R.E. Toronto: McClelland & Stewart, 1958.

Yoneda, Sylvia. "Working For A Living Myth & Fact." *Ridge Reviews*. Mendocino, California: April 1988.

UNPUBLISHED MATERIAL:

Anderson, Andrew. Letter to Honourable Richard McBride, Premier, May 25,1909. BC Provincial Archives Call No. GR 441, V. 34.

British Columbia Archaeological Site Survey Fot'm, Site No. EdSr 1, EdSr 4 and EdSq 13.

British Columbia Archives and Records Service, Maps Division. Call numbers: CM A423 1903, CM B666 1907, CM B639 1908.

British Columbia, Department of Education, Annual Report of Public Schools, 1905. Victoria: 1906.

British Columbia, Department of Education, Annual Report of Public Schools, 1906. Victoria: 1907.

British Columbia Sessional Papers. 1903,1905,1915 and 1917. British Columbia Archives and Records Service. Victoria.

Corker, Rev. A.W. Diary 1889–1890. Alert Bay Library and Museum.

Correspondence between barrister E. Coatsworth of Toronto and T.M. Daly, Minister of the Interior, Ottawa. 1892. National Archives of Canada.

Correspondence between the Secretary of the Department
of Immigration and Henry A. Sherwood. McBride Papers
1905. British Columbia Archives and Records Service.

Duff, Wilson. "The Southern Kwakiutl." Unpublished
manuscript, Archaeology Division, Royal British Columbia
Museum, Victoria, B.C.

Howe, Geordie. "Report of the Vancouver Island Lower
Mainland Cariboo Regional Archaeological Impact
Assessment,1980." Permit 1980: 6. Resource Management
Division, Heritage Conservation Branch, Victoria.

Kuitunen, Alan Neil. "The Finnish Canadian Socialist
Movement 1900–1914." MA Thesis, University of Calgary,
1982.

Letter from Alert Bay Constable Walter Wollacott to the
Honorable Attorney-General, Feb. 24, 1903. British
Columbia Archives and Records Service. Victoria.

Letter from W.M. Halliday to Attorney-General, Jan. 30,
1903. British Columbia Archives and Records Service.
Victoria.

Letter from Matti Kurikka to the Government Secretary
of B.C., May 14, 1901. British Columbia Archives and
Records Service. Victoria.

Lundy, Doris Marion. "The Rock Art of the Northwest
Coast." Simon Fraser University, MA Thesis, December
1974.

Miller, Philip Carl. "A British Columbia Fishing Village.
" University of British Columbia. PhD Thesis in
Interdisciplinary Studies, 1978.

Ministry of Lands and Parks. Victoria, B.C. Land Registers.

Murphy, Mary. "An Economic History of Malcolm Island."
Economics paper. University of Waterloo, 1983.

Murphy, Mary. "Better Lands and A Perfect Home:
Americans in Canada." Senior Essay, Wayne State
University. May 1989.

National Archives of Canada. Finnish Archives, Manuscript
Division. Newspaper clippings, printed articles,
transcripts, notes, 1909–1951. Correspondence, printed
articles, newspaper clippings, memoirs, 1917–1952.
Selected translations.

Oberg, Kalervo. "A History of a Communist Society in British Columbia." University of British Columbia. BA essay in Economics, 1928.

Peltoniemi, Teuvo. "Finnish Utopian Settlements in North America." Proceedings of the Third Finn Forum Congress on Finnish Emigration. Turku, Finland, Sept. 5–8, 1984.

Premier correspondence Inward, no. 280/09 (official) Andrew Anderson to Richard McBride, May 25, 1909. British Columbia Archives and Records Service. Victoria.

Canada Indian Affairs, miscellaneous documents and correspondence. British Columbia Archives and Records Service. Victoria.

Salo, Allan Henry. "The Kalevan Kansa Colonization Company Ltd: A Finnish Millenarian Movement in British Columbia." University of British Columbia. MA Thesis in Anthropology, 1978.

NEWSPAPERS:

The *Aika*. Nanaimo and Sointula. 1901–1905.
The *Colonist*, Victoria, B.C. 1890–1906.
The *Co-operative Consumer*, 1978. Sointula Museum.
The *Daily Herald*, Nanaimo, B.C. 1901
The *Evening Journal*, Ottawa, Ontario. 1899.
The *Fisherman*, Vancouver, B.C. 1959.
The *Ladysmith Chronicle*, Ladysmith, B.C. 1962.
The *Montreal Daily Witness*. Quebec. 1899.
The *North Island Gazette*, Port Hardy, B.C. 1984.
The *Pioneer Journal*, Alert Bay, B.C. 1941–1957.
The *Province*, Vancouver, B.C. 1899–1938.
The *Vancouver Sun*, Vancouver, B.C. 1948–1979.